SIMPLIFIED SITE DESIGN

SIMPLIFIED SITE DESIGN

JAMES AMBROSE

PETER BRANDOW

University of Southern California

A Wiley-Interscience Publication

JOHN WILEY & SONS, INC.

New York • Chichester • Brisbane • Toronto • Singapore

Copyright © 1992 by John Wiley & Sons, Inc.

Library of Congress Cataloging in Publication Data:

Ambrose, James E.
    Simplified site design/James Ambrose, Peter Brandow.
       p.   cm.— (Parker-Ambrose series of simplified design guides)

    Includes bibliographical references and index.

    ISBN 0-471-53029-8
    1. Building sites—Planning. I. Brandow, Peter. II. Title.
III. Series.
TH375.A43 1992
720'.28—dc20   91-26269
                                    CIP

Printed in the United States of America

10 9 8 7 6 5 4 3 2 1

CONTENTS

Preface

This book deals with the many design concerns of building sites. Although the potential scope of this topic is immense, the intent here is to treat it in a concise manner. One means of achieving this is to deal with issues from the general point of view of the site designer, the person with *overall* concern for the site as a designed object. This focus of interest tends to emphasize the broader aspects of planning and design, and those problems of integrating the work of various specialists with the site design as a whole.

The building site represents a conflux of concerns, constantly calling for a broad, multiviewing of issues. One consideration is that the site, as an outdoor space, literally belongs both to the property (and building) owner and users as well as to the neighbors and community at large. Another common problem is the overlapping of interests of various individual design professionals, resulting in the much-needed cooperation among architect, landscape architect, civil engineer, urban planner, and various specialists for utilities, street traffic control, water and flood control, air traffic control, etc.

Within this potential whirlwind of overlapping interests is the basic problem of planning the site and designing its essential features: its finished surface geometry, parking, access points, landscaping, site constructions, and so on. This book focuses on a simple presentation of these basic factors with a concentration on their fundamental issues. The intent is to allow the reader to develop a general view of the most fundamental problems of developing building sites as designed objects.

It is expected that readers may have different backgrounds and different particular interests or goals. We have not aimed the presentations here at a very specific audience, except for the assumption of a general interest in the problems of designing building sites. To help the less experienced reader, we have provided some study aids at the back of the book that can be used in a self-study process to evaluate one's understanding of the book materials.

The authors of this book are experienced in both education and professional work, covering architecture, landscape architecture, and civil engineering. It is hoped that this scope of experience has given us an appreciation of the interests of the expanded family of designers who deal with building sites.

We are grateful to our teachers, professional colleagues, students, and design clients. These interactions have enabled us to view more sympathetically the learning process and the professional design experience.

JAMES AMBROSE
PETER BRANDOW

October 1991

About the Authors

James Ambrose has served on the faculties of three architecture schools and has many years of experience in professional practice as an architect and as a structural engineer. He is the author of several books, including the recent second edition of *Simplified Foundation Design* and the recent second edition of Parker and MacGuire, *Simplified Site Engineering.* He is currently a member of the faculty of the School of Architecture at the University of Southern California in Los Angeles.

Peter Brandow is an architect and landscape architect with more than 25 years of professional experience in site and landscape design for projects throughout the United States and Central America. He was for several years an associate partner of the prominent landscape design firm of Emmett Wemple and Associates in Los Angeles and is now in private practice in Costa Mesa, California. He is a part time member of the faculty of the Department of Civil Engineering at the University of Southern California.

1

INTRODUCTION

The general problem of site design involves the overlapping of a number of technical fields and separate design professionals. What needs to be done and who does it vary considerably for different buildings and different sites. In dense, urban situations, sites are often virtually invisible, consisting essentially of the building footprint. On the other hand, large, open, fully developed sites may represent site design work that overwhelms the building design problem (see Figure 1.1).

1.1 WHAT IS SITE DESIGN?

In general, site design entails the whole range of concerns relating to the development, or redevelopment, of a piece of ground for some planned purpose. One assumed purpose is the construction of a building on the site. There are thus many building/site relations and interactions relating to direct physical connections and sharing of the site space. However, there are also many site issues to be dealt with outside the building, particularly with large sites, related groups of buildings, and the many concerns for the site edges as transitions to surrounding spaces.

In this book, we do not attempt to clearly identify professional design fields, but choose rather to concentrate on the problems of design. Many specific tasks are often targeted for particular professionals: for example, soils investigation to the geotechnical specialists, foundation design to the structural en-

(a)

(b)

FIGURE 1.1 Building sites: (a) typical urban condition with the site almost fully covered by the building; (b) rural site with the building in a parklike setting.

gineer, building design to the architect. However, for general site design, there is likely to be project-by-project negotiation as to who performs what tasks and who maintains overall control of the site design.

1.2 SCOPE OF THIS BOOK

This book deals quite comprehensively with the general problem of designing sites for buildings. Space limitations and the general spirit of the ''Simplified Series'' (of which this book is a part) are the primary parameters for defining coverage of this subject, in addition to which this book is one of three books that treat related topics.

Simplified Design of Building Foundations discusses the general problems of developing the in-ground construction base for buildings. While this is a major aspect of building design, it is also related very intimately with the general concerns for the use of the building site. Critically overlapping issues are dealt with here, in some cases borrowing materials from the foundations book. However, the reader is referred to that book for more comprehensive treatment of the broad topic of building foundations and the structural aspects of soil behavior.

Simplified Site Engineering for Architects and Builders, Second Edition, treats the basic issues of site analysis, surveying, grading, mapping, surface drainage, and the general scope of work ordinarily identified with the role of the civil engineer. Again, many overlapping topics are covered here, with that book cited as a reference in certain situations.

Simplified Site Design is viewed as the keystone of this three-book set. It encompasses the whole topic of sites in the broadest manner, but limits discussion of specific problems more appropriately and more fully developed in the other two books.

There are many other useful references for the various concerns of site design. The principal ones used in the development of this book are listed in the References section at the end of the text. These, as well as other more specific references, are cited frequently throughout the book for those who wish to pursue individual topics in greater depth.

1.3 HOW TO USE THIS BOOK

Since the purpose of this book is to provide a relatively concise treatment, an introduction to the topic of site design, the book materials are presented in a sequence that permits a general development of the subject in a logical, progressive order. However, a specific topic of interest can be selected for reading without complete dependence on what preceded it.

Considerable citation of other sources of information is made throughout the book to facilitate further study of individual topics. Those readers desiring to become more familiar with the subject are advised to use the Glossary to build their general vocabulary; the learning of terms and their meaning helps build a better idea of their overall significance and the ideas they represent.

Readers with interest in serious study should examine the materials in the Study Aids section. These are intended for use in an organized study program that tests the reader's accomplishments at various stages in the reading of the book.

1.4 UNITS: SYSTEMS

Measurement of length, area, and volume are in feet and inches, and various correlated units such as yards, miles, and acres. Conversions between these units and the metric-based units of the SI (Systeme International) system must frequently be performed in professional design work. Persons seeking to obtain work in site engineering should expect to encounter these problems and should become familiar with the necessary conversion procedure.

At the time of preparation of this edition, the building industry in the United States is still in a state of confused transition from the use of English units

Table 1.1   UNITS OF MEASUREMENT: U.S. SYSTEM

Name of Unit	Abbreviation	Use
Length		
Foot	ft.	Large dimensions, building plans, beam spans
Inch	in.	Small dimensions, size of member cross sections
Area		
Square feet	ft^2	Large areas
Square inches	$in.^2$	Small areas, properties of cross sections
Volume		
Cubic feet	ft^3	Large volumes, quantities of materials
Cubic inches	$in.^3$	Small volumes
Force, Mass		
Pound	lb	Specific weight, force, load
Kip	k	1000 lb
Pounds per foot	lb/ft	Linear load (as on a beam)
Kips per foot	k/ft	Linear load (as on a beam)
Pounds per square foot	lb/ft^2, psf	Distributed load on a surface
Kips per square foot	k/ft^2, ksf	Distributed load on a surface
Pounds per cubic foot	lb/ft^3, pcf	Relative density, weight
Moment		
Foot-pounds	ft-lb	Rotational or bending moment
Inch-pounds	in.-lb	Rotational or bending moment
Kip-feet	k-ft	Rotational or bending moment
Kip-inches	k-in.	Rotational or bending moment
Stress		
Pounds per square foot	lb/ft^2, psf	Soil pressure
Pounds per square inch	$lb/in.^2$, psi	Stresses in structures
Kips per square foot	k/ft^2, ksf	Soil pressure
Kips per square inch	$k/in.^2$, ksi	Stresses in structures
Temperature		
Degree Fahrenheit	°F	Temperature

(feet, pounds, etc.) to the new metric-based SI units. Although a complete phase-over to the SI system seems inevitable, most U.S. suppliers of construction materials and products are still resistant. (The old system is now more appropriately called the U.S. system because England no longer uses it.)

For readers who need to make conversions between the two systems, there are three tables provided here. Table 1.1 lists the standard units of measurement in the U.S. system with the abbreviations generally used in this book and a description of their use in engineering work. In similar form, Table 1.2 gives the corresponding information in the SI system. The conversion factors used in shifting from one system to the other are provided in Table 1.3.

Table 1.2   UNITS OF MEASUREMENT: SI SYSTEM

Name of Unit	Abbreviation	Use
Length		
Meter	m	Large dimensions, building plans, beam spans
Millimeter	mm	Small dimensions, size of member cross sections
Area		
Square meters	m^2	Large areas
Square millimeters	mm^2	Small areas, properties of cross sections
Volume		
Cubic meters	m^3	Large volumes
Cubic millimeters	mm^3	Small volumes
Mass		
Kilogram	kg	Mass of materials (equivalent to weight in U.S. system)
Kilograms per cubic meter	kg/m^3	Density
Force (Load on Structures)		
Newton	N	Force or load
Kilonewton	kN	1000 newtons
Stress		
Pascal	Pa	Stress or pressure (1 pascal = $1\ N/m^2$)
Kilopascal	kPa	1000 pascal
Megapascal	MPa	1,000,000 pascal
Gigapascal	GPa	1,000,000,000 pascal
Temperature		
Degree Celsius	°C	Temperature

Table 1.3 FACTORS FOR CONVERSION OF UNITS

To Convert from U.S. Units to SI Units, Multiply by:	U.S. Unit	SI Unit	To Convert from SI Units to U.S. Units, Multiply by:
25.4	in.	mm	0.03937
0.3048	ft	m	3.281
645.2	in.^{2}	mm^2	1.550×10^{-3}
16.39×10^3	in.^{3}	mm^3	61.02×10^{-6}
416.2×10^3	in.^{4}	mm^4	2.403×10^{-4}
0.09290	ft^2	m^2	10.76
0.02832	ft^3	m^3	35.31
0.4536	lb (mass)	kg	2.205
4.448	lb (force)	N	0.2248
4.448	kip (force)	kN	0.2248
1.356	ft-lb (moment)	N-m	0.7376
1.356	kip-ft (moment)	kN-m	0.7376
1.488	lb/ft (mass)	kg/m	0.6720
14.59	lb/ft (load)	N/m	0.06853
14.59	kips/ft (load)	kN/m	0.06853
6.895	psi (stress)	kPa	0.1450
6.895	ksi (stress)	MPa	0.1450
0.04788	psf (load or pressure)	kPa	20.93
47.88	ksf (load or pressure)	kPa	0.02093
16.02	pcf (density)	kg/m^3	0.06242
$0.566 \times (°F - 32)$	°F	°C	$(1.8 \times °C) + 32$

1.5 UNITS: USAGE

Notation of quantities for length, area, and volume may be done in different ways. In this book, two methods are used to indicate length. The first uses feet and decimal parts of a foot; thus four and one-half feet is noted as 4.5 ft. This form is generally used for computational work and on most engineering drawings.

The second method of linear measurement uses feet and inches and fractional parts of inches. Thus four and one-half feet is noted as 4 ft 6 in.; frequently recorded with shorthand notation as 4'6". This form of notation is frequently used on architectural and construction drawings.

Angular measurement in this book is done with the angle-degree-minute system for recording information on drawings. However, for computations, it is usually necessary to convert to a decimal fraction system, indicating fractions of one degree as a decimal; thus an angle of 12 and one-third degrees is expressed as 12.33 degrees. Older surveying equipment, maps, and data references tend to use the degree-minute-second system, while newer work is mostly done with the decimal fractions, which streamline much more directly with computational procedures. A familiarity with both systems is necessary, and in most cases conversions are cases quite simple.

1.6 SYMBOLS

The following "shorthand" symbols are frequently used:

Symbol	Reading	Symbol	Reading
>	greater than	6′	6 feet
<	less than	6″	6 inches
≥	equal to or greater than	Σ	the sum of
≤	equal to or less than	ΔL	change in L

1.7 NOTATION AND ABBREVIATIONS

The following notations and abbreviations are used throughout this book. Where standards are widely used, they are generally applied here. Care should be exercised when using many references, as there is often a lack of standard usage of notation and abbreviations. Special note should be made of usage in building codes, which often provide quite specific definition. In general, the notation and abbreviations used here comply with those in the *Uniform Building Code* (Ref. 12).

a = increment of an area (ft^2, in.^{2}, etc.)
A = gross area (ft^2, in.^{2}, etc.)
D = diameter
e = eccentricity, as a dimension of mislocation of something
f = computed unit stress (psi, psf, etc.)
F = (1) force; (2) allowable unit stress
h = height, as a measured distance
H = horizontal component of a force
l = length dimension
L = length dimension
N = number of
p = unit pressure, as compressive stress or force
P = concentrated load (force at a point)
R = radius
s = spacing dimension, usually center-to-center of a set of objects
t = thickness dimension
T = temperature
w = (1) width dimension; (2) unit weight
W = gross weight
Δ (delta) = change of
θ (theta) = angle
Σ (sigma) = sum of
ϕ (phi) = angle

2

ASPECTS OF SITE DESIGN

The complete development of a building site is often a complicated task involving many people and competing concerns. This chapter presents some discussions aimed at identifying these issues and clarifying just what it is that site design amounts to.

2.1 SITE DEVELOPMENT

In its broadest sense, this topic has many aspects, ordinarily involving the concerns of many designers. The general form, functional problems, and appearance of building sites are problems of major concern to architects, but also to planners, landscape architects, civil engineers, and other professionals.

Items on and below the ground surface of a site are of concern to the site development, the building, and the various building utilities and services. Many individual designers must deal with these items, but the whole effort must be carefully coordinated if chaos is to be avoided.

Design coordination is further complicated by the fact that the first work on the site, which often precedes completion of much of the design work, is the regrading and excavation necessary to begin construction and install the unseen site infrastructure (what we will later call the *invisible site*). In many ways, the scheduling and sequences of design work, construction work, contract negotiations, financial development, and building agency approvals do not mesh well.

2.2 CONCERNS FOR SITE DEVELOPMENT

While appearance and general spatial functioning of sites are critical concerns, there are many other design considerations for sites, including the following:

Site traffic circulation; pedestrians and autos.

Surface drainage and disposal of runoff water

Development of plantings and the general landscape design

Placement of the building on the site

Development of building foundations and below-grade construction

Connections to off-site services

Site edge interface with existing streets and properties

Site lighting, both natural and artificial

Sound, for privacy and general noise control

Air quality, as affected by building exhaust air, site auto traffic, etc.

Fire safety, in terms of exiting building occupants and building and site access by firefighters

Security for people and contents of buildings

The shaping and general constructing of building sites must respond to all of these concerns—and, in many situations, to various additional ones.

The primary topic of this book is site development in general, but the site for a building must work with the building. Thus, the selection of materials, components, systems, and details for site construction impinge on the work of the designers of every aspect of the building and site. While it is occasionally necessary to concentrate on only a few concerns, or even a single one, all of the potential affects of choices for the construction must eventually be dealt with and coordinated.

While the building site is of itself a definable place and a specific design concern, it must also relate to the general building enclosure, access to the building, entry to the building, and the many building service systems. In the end, the whole building and its site must be designed, even though specific situations may be dealt with as individual problems.

The point of view here is that of the designer and what is of primary concern in the design process. The writing of specifications, management of construction, and production of materials and components for construction are necessary activities that will be considered, but design is the focus.

2.3 DIVISION OF SITE DESIGN WORK

Typically many people are involved in any site development. These include the owner or purchaser of the site, the various designers who work with the site, the contractors who do site and building construction work, and the local authorities and agencies who control the type of work planned for the site.

Work for site development typically overlaps the interests of many designers and consultants (see Figure 2.1). Site design activities are not always clearly divided among the major design professionals, resulting in work that often overlaps their spheres of action. For small projects, the primary design professional (usually an architect, landscape architect, or civil engineer) may do all or almost all of the site design work. On large projects, however, the design work is usually shared by many specialists, requiring considerable coordination and management.

Activities related to site development typically include the following:

Surveys and Investigations. This includes studies of the existing surface conditions and site features; subsurface materials and geology; setbacks,

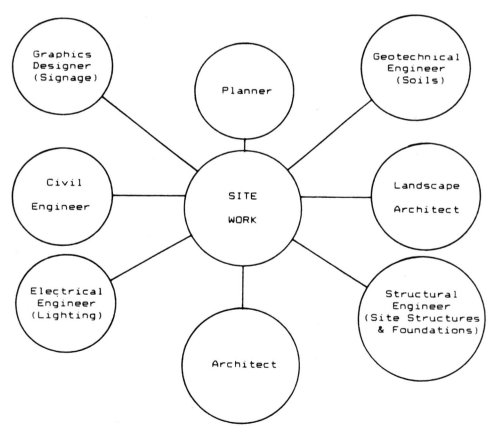

FIGURE 2.1 Site design as a conflux of activities of many design professionals

easements, and other legal constraints; and any special studies for seismology, water conditions, slope stability, etc.

Site Engineering. This includes the general recontouring of the site surface, design for control of site drainage and any required surface stabilization, planning for site construction (pavements, retaining walls, etc.), general planning for utilities and services (sewers, water, and other underground elements), and development of the site edges to relate to existing streets and properties.

Landscape Design. General usage and development of the site, including use of plant materials and various constructed elements for the visible site.

Foundation Design. The general design for the below-grade portions of the buildings and the supporting foundations.

Design for Site Construction Work. The necessary planning for excavation, temporary shoring, dewatering, and other work related to achieving the site and below-grade construction work.

All of this activity must be well coordinated by the prime site design professional. This involves ensuring that all the work is done, that individual specialists do not duplicate each other's work or develop conflicts, and that the work proceeds in a well-scheduled manner.

2.4 THE MICRO-SITE: INTERNAL CONCERNS

Most of what is actually accomplished in site design work deals with the site itself. The design output is essentially a restatement of conditions for the site. However, there are inputs to the design work that stem from concerns for potential situations both within and beyond the site boundaries.

This section deals with issues that arise from conditions within the site boundaries, what we call the *micro-site*. This includes the existing site, the building that will occupy the site, and the general development of the internal site (see Figure 2.2).

For the existing site—that is, the site as it is before any construction work begins—performing a complete survey of the existing conditions is of primary importance. This process and the various forms of information typically required are described more fully in Chapter 3. Major concerns involve:

The general site surface form, called the site *topology*.

Existing physical elements on the site, such as trees, rock outcroppings, streams, or buildings, with particular concern for elements that may be desirable to preserve, protect, or feature.

The character of surface and near-surface soils, as affects their potential for use in redevelopment of the site surface, for landscaping or for the support of pavements or other site construction.

FIGURE 2.2 Development of the site interior as a captive space

The character of deep subsurface soils, relating to the development of the
   building foundations and other deep-seated construction.
Any existing underground elements, such as utility lines, sewers, tunnels,
   etc.
Any legal restrictions within the site boundaries, such as easements, setbacks, height restrictions, etc.

Design of the site—and in many ways the design of the building for the
site—must begin with consideration of these existing conditions, as early decisions are those for the placement of the building on the site, both horizontally and vertically, and any major reshaping of the site surface. All the items
listed above can affect the feasibility of proposals for these major design concerns.

2.5 THE MACRO-SITE: EXTENDED ENVIRONMENTS

While what gets primarily manipulated in site design is the site itself, there
are always major concerns for the world outside the site, what we call the

FIGURE 2.3 The site as a visually shared neighborhood object.

macro-site. This begins with considerations for the development of the site edges or boundaries (see Figure 2.3).

The site edges represent the terminal limits of the internal site development. They also represent the immediate *interfaces of the site* with surrounding properties and elements such as streets, alleys, river banks, lake shorelines, and so on. In most instances, the edges represent fixed conditions generally not subject to major redevelopment. For instance, it may be possible to obtain permission for a curb cut to install a driveway on the site, but vertical or horizontal relocation of a bounding street or adjacent natural feature is much less likely.

In most situations, edges will establish major design constraints for the general site design, often including concerns for some of the following items.

Recontouring of the Site. Edges might be shaped by property line walls or other structures, but in general the reshaping must be accomplished entirely internally, with edges being fixed conditions.

Site Surface Drainage. Whether the site is in the desert or the tropics, site drainage has a major impact on the development of site form. Just about any work on a site will affect existing drainage of the site surface. This must be carefully analyzed for any design proposals and the affects on properties at the site edges given major attention. Agencies issuing permits for site work or building construction will be very attentive to this concern.

Access to the Site. Sites must usually be accessed from their edges, whether this refers to pedestrian traffic, vehicular traffic, utility services, or sewers. Management of these items on the site may be subject to some manipulation, but the access at the site edges is usually considerably constrained.

Building and Site Orientation. What exists at the various edges of the site is quite likely to affect the general orientation for planning of the site and any buildings on it. Streets, shorelines, existing structures, and other elements occurring at edges are sure to require major consideration. Views from and into the site must be considered. Orientation to the sun and general weather exposure are also important factors.

Beyond the site edges, of course, is the rest of the world, beginning with the adjacent properties. The limits for concern here are mostly a matter for the judgment of designers, although some considerations may be imposed.

If the immediate environment outside the site is very pleasant, it will usually be desirable to make both the site and the building a part of that environment. The site may be developed in real continuity with the general environment; the building may be very outward-oriented, with lots of windows permitting involvement of the building occupants with the outdoors.

On the other hand, it may be necessary to deal with both the site and the building as very private, inward-focusing situations when the general exterior environment is hostile, unaccommodating, or downright ugly. This does not sound very community-minded, but is sometimes a simple matter of practicality, especially in urban situations.

Many sites have some good and some bad edges, requiring some orientation for both the site and building planning work (see Figure 2.4). For the building, this may relate to the existence of good views from windows. It may also relate to some of the elements that are both building- and site-related, such as balconies, decks, patios, play-yards, entry walks, and driveways.

Emerging concerns, and increasing actual code requirements, for energy conservation and solar access make the recognition of these factors increasingly critical for design work. The effects of tall trees or constructed objects in providing either desired sheltering or unwanted blocking of sun or wind may be critical on the site or for adjacent neighbors.

FIGURE 2.4 Good edges and bad edges—shared for good times and bad

The essential idea here is to keep in mind that the site has a larger context that embraces its total surroundings, in most situations extending well beyond the site boundaries.

2.6 BUILDING/SITE RELATIONS

Sites for buildings must be developed with major concerns for the site-to-building relationships. Some of these fundamental concerns are the routes of access to the building entry points, the placement and orientation of the building on the site, the development of the building base and foundations, and the connections to services, particularly those underground.

Beyond these basic functional relations, the significant concerns become related to the general character of the site, the neighborhood environment, and the function of the site as a significant space unto itself. For constrictive site situations, where the building footprint virtually blots out the site, there may be little site development beyond the functional aspects just mentioned.

When sites are large and the building occupies a small portion of the total site area, the site design may be a major activity unto itself, with the building representing a minor design problem, although possibly one of major significance.

Many aspects of building/site relations from a design point of view depend on the designers' attitudes or philosophies. Buildings may be designed with minimal concern for their sites, with the site design executed as an afterthought, on a par with interior decoration. In a better world, however, the site is developed as one with the building, both functionally and philosophically.

Building/site relations are discussed more fully in Chapter 5.

2.7 WHOSE SITE IS IT?

A philosophical argument to be dealt with in developing an approach to site design is that of the real ownership of the site. Of course, legal title to a site is vested in the legal owner of the property and certainly implies some major rights of true ownership. However, many sites and buildings are owned by people or organizations that do not use them, and the real ''owners'' from a design point of view may be questionable from the designer's point of view.

Site development must be considered as an investment and pursued with the property owner's best interests. However, many aspects of design must relate to the functional needs of the actual users: children, for example, for an elementary school. A good-looking appearance to enhance property values is a worthwhile intention, but satisfying the needs of the users is also significant.

As outdoor spaces, sites also ''belong'' to all those people who experience them as such, whether only visually or for actual use. Walking or driving past

FIGURE 2.5 Sites are sometimes truly shared with others

or through a site every day makes anyone a partial user of the site with some vested interests (see Figure 2.5).

Many sites are continuous in form with adjacent properties, creating a larger ''site,'' or a true macro-site of some kind. Developed residential neighborhoods are often of this nature, with sites merging into a single, general texture of the larger landscape. In such cases, a single site becomes an artificial element, with true existence known only by map outlines and legal descriptions.

Most designers feel this way about sites, that they are parts of a continuum and relate to a larger context, even though some individuality may be desired for the owner, the users, or the designer's personal statement. This is not necessarily a social or political attitude, but usually simply a concession to the larger context for design. However, there is also a trend today for communities and advocacy groups to promote this approach in a more legally binding way, through the use of building codes, zoning ordinances, and establishment of review boards for proposed work.

3

DETERMINATION OF SITE CONDITIONS

Preceding any real design solutions for a site there must be a thorough investigation of the site and collection of various forms of information. For building sites, this is likely to be done as part of a general predesign analysis. However, even in such cases, the site is one of the earliest areas for concern, since it is likely to yield many issues and constraints for the building design. This chapter pursues the general concerns for information about sites that are likely to affect the design work.

3.1 THE EXISTING SITE

Existing site conditions present a situation for the site designer similar to that of a blank canvas for a painter. The conditions may be totally natural for previously undeveloped sites, or a completely developed heritage from previous owners or users of the site.

For various reasons, there may be a predisposition to leave the site in its present condition as much as possible. This may be due to the fact that it is a beautiful site, whether a natural one or a developed one. If it is essentially functionally usable as is, the principal design goal may be to make as little intrusion or change as possible. This may also be a matter of economics in some situations.

Of course, building a new building on the site or modifying an old one is likely to effect some changes. If nothing else, the performing of the construction work is likely to disturb the site significantly. If the intent is truly to disturb the site as little as possible, the efforts required to preserve existing site features or elements may become a major design activity.

At the other extreme, it may be desirable, or even necessary, to completely redevelop the site. In this event, it may be even more critical to thoroughly investigate and document the existing conditions. This generally calls for a complete site inventory and an evaluation of which features or elements need to be changed or removed, what can be preserved or recycled, and so on. No item on the site can be ignored in this design situation.

3.2 THE DESIGN PROBLEM

Preliminary investigation of sites should be done with some idea of the general design intentions. This makes for a sort of chicken and egg situation, since some simple information about the site must be used for any realistic design projections.

In reality, what is usually required is some sequential investigation, with some very early simple investigations used for preliminary design studies and a more thorough followup investigation once more specific design intentions have been established. If the site is reasonably accessible, there are likely to be many site visits during the design work, as the need for more precise information emerges.

Some design problems may be forthcoming merely on the basis of information about the site. The need to remedy some situations or deal with exceptionally constraining ones may strongly influence the feasibility of design solutions for a site. This is typically the case in areas that are already intensely developed, with existing streets, utilities, neighboring properties, and many legal constraints requiring setbacks, height restrictions, easements, etc.

Anyone with some design experience knows that design work hardly ever flows in a clean, linear process, regardless of the experience of designers or careful management of the design process. The points to be made here are that no design work should be undertaken to any extent without some preliminary information, and no expensive, extensive investigation should be undertaken until some preliminary design intentions are defined. In addition, once the design work is underway, some interplay between design work and investigation for information should be expected.

3.3 INFORMATION FOR THE PHYSICAL SITE

Whenever the development of a site is planned some information about the site is required. The type and extent of information may vary, depending both on site conditions and the type of planned development. The general process of gathering information is sometimes described as *surveying* the site, although the actual work of surveying is itself a special process of finding specific horizontal and vertical dimensions. Information determined by surveying and other investigations is often displayed on a map (or plan) of the site.

Site Surveys

The term *site survey* is usually reserved for a special map that is produced by a professional *land surveyor* and is registered with local authorities as a legal document that becomes part of the legal description of the property. (See Figure 3.1.) However, the specific legal definition of a site is contained in a written description of the property that refers to its location based on the established legal boundaries of the region (city, county, etc.).

In addition to the site boundaries, a survey indicates various other information, such as:

Locations of adjacent streets and alleys

Easements for utilities (portions of the property that have existing utilities or are held available for future installations)

Locations and descriptions of major site features, such as ponds, streams, rock outcroppings, existing buildings, large trees, etc.

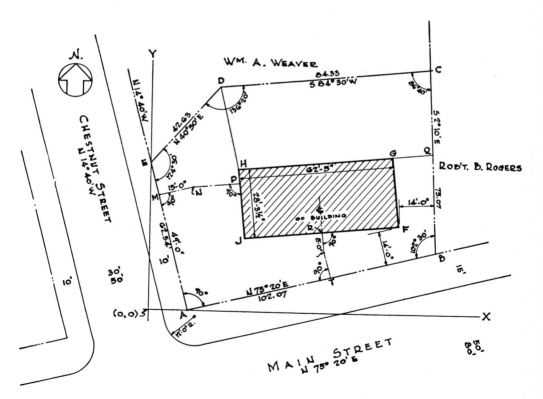

FIGURE 3.1 Typical form of a site survey

The site survey is a general description of the site, with an emphasis on surface features.

Other information about a site may be useful, or specifically required, for the planning of site development. Additional types, sources, and uses of information include the following:

General Area Map. These may be obtained from local authorities, various agencies (highway, agriculture, U.S. Army, etc.), or commercial mapping services.

Geographic Statistics. These maps display distribution of various data, such as population density, air pollution, seismicity, snow or rainfall, wind, degree days, etc.

Aerial Surveys (Photo Maps). These exist for many regions of the United States and are generally obtainable from government agencies or commercial mapping services.

Geotechnical Surveys. These deal with information on ground conditions and geological properties of the surface and subsurface ground materials. Some existing information may be available from general surveys made by agencies or from studies for previous site development. Obtaining a permit for any site development usually requires the performing of such a survey prior to any construction activity.

In any area where considerable development already exists, a great deal of information is usually available regarding the general conditions of the site region. This information can be used, together with a visit to the site, to get a preview of site conditions.

The exact type and extent of new information required for the planning and development of a site will depend on the nature of the planned work, specific requirements of local government agencies, unique site conditions, and amount of existing information.

Maps

Geographical information, legal property descriptions, and site surveys of various kinds are generally related to the production of maps. Maps are essentially horizontal, planar views of some region of the earth's surface. Data may be recorded directly on the map or refer to some identified portion of the map.

The making of maps, called *cartography*, is a highly developed science that uses quite specific procedures and forms of data. Any references to internationally established latitudes or longitudes, to boundaries of countries, states, counties, or municipalities, or to legally defined private properties must follow carefully defined procedures.

In addition, forms of information such as locations of streets and highways, established survey references (such as benchmarks, Section 8.4), height re-

strictions for construction, or property easements must be displayed in established formats.

Site Development Plans

In general, maps are produced and used in highly controlled situations. Plans,
on the other hand, are developed for specific purposes, and the form, as well
as the type of information displayed, relate to the type of activity for which
the plans are prepared. For site development, the frequently used types of
plans are listed below.

Site Plan. This is essentially a site map, typically created for some actual
mapping purposes. The result is a repetition of data from site surveys,
but also a display of various aspects of the proposed work. (See Figure
3.2.) For simple projects a single plot plan may suffice. For large, complex projects, a series of plans may display selected information for
greater readability. The plot plans are typically part of the set of construction drawings for a construction project.

Grading Plan. This is generally a site map that displays the existing site
contours (form of the surface) and existing features (such as trees, existing construction, etc.); it also indicates the form of the recontoured
and generally redeveloped site surface, called the *finished grade*. As a

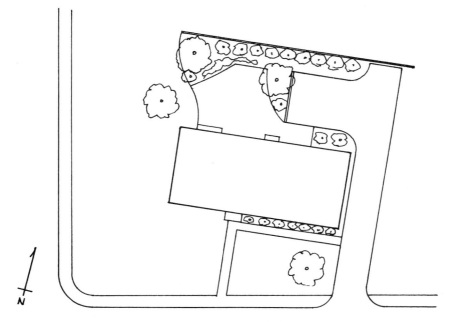

FIGURE 3.2 Site plan, indicating proposed landscape development for the site in
Figure 3.1.

separate drawing, a grading plan is prepared specifically to inform the workers responsible for recontouring the site surface. For completion of the site design work, the grading plan shows the *finished grade*, which is the final site surface.

Construction Plans. These are plans showing the horizontal planar view of the construction work proposed for a site. The construction itself will typically be additionally described with various detailed drawings. Separate plans may be drawn for site construction (drives, curbs, retaining structures, planters, etc.), building foundations, other below-grade construction (basements, tunnels, etc.), and the grade level (first floor) of proposed buildings.

Data Sources

Generally, maps are used primarily as data sources in the design process for site and building development. They describe an ''as is'' condition, from which plans may be developed for proposed work. Within the site boundaries, changes can be made with some freedom, although practical and legal restrictions are usually limiting factors.

Site development is constrained by many aspects of the boundary conditions. The simple dimensions of boundaries must be recognized, resulting in a limit on the extent of horizontal projection of the construction. However, many other aspects of planning must recognize boundaries and adjacent features. The following are some specific concerns.

Surface Drainage. Recontouring of the site, as well as new construction, must not cause problems for adjacent properties in terms of rechannelling surface water drainage during rainfalls.

Existing Streets, etc. These usually represent unchangeable conditions that must be dealt with in recontouring, planning drives, and so on. Vehicular entry and exit on the site must recognize traffic conditions and other restrictions of existing elements.

Existing Utilities. Connections to existing services (for power, water, gas, phones, etc.) must usually be made with recognition of existing mains. Of special concern are sewers, which work by gravity drainage, making vertical location of on-site elements critical.

Adjacent Properties. Construction on the site must not jeopardize adjacent properties or present the dangers of undermining, erosion, etc. Many communities now also control issues such as blocking of sunlight, views, or prevailing winds for existing properties.

A major purpose of the survey is to establish all the data necessary for an informed design that recognizes all these concerns, as well as others appropriate to the proposed work or adjacent conditions.

Information for Design Development

Design of construction projects proceeds in a somewhat staggered fashion. At the earliest stages, very broad decisions are made without detailed information. Detailed information must usually be obtained on the basis of some actual design studies (preliminary design developments) so that the purpose of the detailed information (such as geotechnical surveys) is specifically determined.

Thus, the generation of information to support the design work and the design work itself must be developed in a stepped procedure. First, some general information and then some preliminary design; next, some more specific information and then some more definitive design; then some very critical, special information, and so on. This process may actually continue into and through the construction work, since some information may only be obtainable during the actual redeveloping of the site (what is down there below the ground surface at some specific point on the site).

It is important to anticipate the need for information at various stages of design, recognize the feasibility of obtaining various forms of information, and plan for the general flow and interchange of design work and information gathering. In the best of situations, design work will not proceed uninformed and information will be obtained in a proper and timely fashion.

3.4 GENERAL INFORMATION

While the clear definition of the existing physical site is highly important, there are often other forms of information also required for site design. This situation varies considerably for different sites, different regions, and different site or building designs. Some common forms of information follow.

Negotiated Property Usage Restrictions. These include items that may be mentioned in the title description or included in the title search documents. However, some restrictions may be negotiated on a large tract basis that apply to all individual properties in the tract.

Zoning Ordinances, etc. Many sites are restricted by zoning ordinances or other actions imposed by legislative bodies or government agencies. Chasing down all those that apply to a single site can be a real chore, one usually assigned to lawyers or consultants specializing in this.

Weather and General Climate Records. These yield information on annual rainfall, depth of frost penetration, temperature extremes, prevailing winds, risk of windstorms, probability of earthquakes, etc.

Regional Demographic Studies. These provide a variety of information regarding local conditions, both existing and projected. These studies are likely to be more important to the general development of the building project as a whole, and may also affect some specific site design issues.

General Community or Regional Development Plans. Just about every government entity—city, town, state—has a "master plan" these days. They are subject to a good deal of modification and no small amount of situational expediencies, but must be acknowledged as a necessity to be dealt with. Preserving local culturally significant buildings, maintaining general community appearances, and working with no-growth policies can prove to be very constraining elements for designers.

In general, anything that has the potential for restricting the freedom of development of a site can be regarded as critical information. Development of drainage patterns, use of irrigation for plantings, placement of structures on property lines, vehicular traffic on and off the site, and many other features can be affected. In some situations, the entire feasibility of a project may be in question where extensive and highly restrictive constraints exist.

3.5 LEGAL CONSTRAINTS

Use of land in the United States is highly controlled. For every buildable site there are a number of sources of legal control on the use of the land itself and any construction to be done on it. Some major sources are described below.

Title of Ownership

Land not owned by the government is owned by individuals or private organizations and secured by a title of ownership. Part of the title is a legal description of the property that establishes the precise location of the property and the basis of ownership.

A major point established by the title is the identification of the *property lines*, which are manifested by lines on a map defining the edges or *boundaries* of the property. The site, as a piece of the surface of the earth, is essentially defined by these map lines.

Usage Restrictions

Just about any piece of property deserving of a legal description also has various restrictions on its use. A primary restriction involves fundamental usage, described as residential, commercial, light manufacturing, and so on. These basic designations then carry with them a whole set of restrictions for that specific use.

Although individual properties must adhere to some designated usage classification, the broad usage controls are typically assigned to large groups of sites. Individual usage can sometimes be renegotiated, but the broader interests of the controlling political unit (city, county, etc.) must be taken into account.

Building Codes

Actual construction on a site is usually controlled by a *building code*, enacted as an ordinance by the political body having jurisdiction over the property. Permission to build on the site must be obtained by submitting detailed descriptions of the proposed construction (typically the same documents used for a contract with a builder). If plans are approved, a *building permit* is issued for the construction.

Proposals for buildings and general site construction must comply with the applicable requirements of the building code. Codes are published for reference use, but are subject to ongoing revision. The code actually in force at the moment of the permit issuing is the applicable one. Individual codes are usually based largely on so-called *model codes*, such as the *Uniform Building Code* (Ref. 12).

Codes typically provide for minimally acceptable construction—that is, the proposed work must be *at least* as good as that required by the code. For basic economic reasons, much construction sufficiently satisfies the codes; it is just barely adequate. Really *good* construction, or *optimal* construction, is seldom achieved by cutting close to the code minimums.

The basic interest of code writers and enforcers is the protection of the safety and welfare of the public. This simply means trying to keep things from falling down, blowing away, burning too easily and quickly, and so on. The concepts of value and enhanced quality are not code considerations.

In addition to these basic sources, there are many other legally enforceable ones, involving health concerns, firefighting concerns, energy use, water use, sun access, air rights, mineral rights, and so on. The bottom line for the site designer is what really significantly affects the reshaping and development of the site. This is not always easy to determine precisely, but it is typically a small fraction of the total of the defined limitations.

3.6 ANALYSIS OF CONDITIONS

Before beginning any phase of design work—from the earliest to the final—it is best to make some analysis of the basic conditions of the design. This includes both the various sources of constraint and the basic premises for specific design goals and objectives. The most clever design work will be invalid if it violates some critical code requirement or badly misses some basic design goal.

Some designers use checklists to regularly assure themselves that their creative efforts are not off target. This mechanistic process may somewhat squelch the creative juices, but then designing sites and buildings is not really a pure, unfettered artistic activity.

Examples of checklists are given in Appendix B. These present the most ordinary and generally minimal conerns; any real situation or highly complex project is likely to add many additional special concerns. Since checking should be a repetitive process, the lists are developed for three stages of design, implying what should be established before proceeding with that work as well as what should be used to analyze its value upon completion.

4

SITE PLANNING

The planning of sites is a general activity involving aspects of engineering, landscape design, and, for building sites, some architectural design. Many of the issues involved have been discussed in Chapter 2. This chapter treats some of the fundamental planning concerns that directly create the typical site design problem.

4.1 DEFINING THE SITE DESIGN PROBLEM

Just what constitutes a ''problem'' for site design must be carefully explored on the basis of the various existing conditions and the design goals for the site. Usually, the first problem to be considered is how to get a building on the site and which site situations may present constraint or difficulty in this regard.

The site may accommodate a building easily or may offer some challenging problems. Any exceptional physical design problems should be confronted very early so that the feasibility of achieving specific building designs for the site can be tested. An extreme shape change of the site or the need for very special foundations can add major costs to a project and may severely limit the budget for the construction of the building itself.

Various external conditions may also present problems to be solved. Lack of paved streets, a local sewer system, power lines, or other services can add other complications to the project. Handling of situations regarding neighboring properties may limit work on the site or even add the necessity to shield construction or erect buffer zones or other means of separation.

Local ordinances, zoning boards, and other sources of legal restrictions may pose severe constraints of various kinds, affecting plans for the significant change of land forms or the development of any major construction. Removal, or even severe trimming, of large trees may be restricted or prohibited by local ordinances.

In the end, the owners and designers of a site must establish their own goals and objectives, incorporating the intentions for use of the property and the accommodation of the various constraints. Site planning problems may exist inherently or be generated by proposed usages.

If proposed designs are to be effectively evaluated, the goals and objectives for the design should be stated as clearly as possible at the outset. This both sets a course for the design work as an informed action and provides for real testing of proposals.

The remaining sections of this chapter deal with various specific considerations for site planning.

4.2 TRAFFIC

Site planning often involves the management of considerable traffic, both pedestrian and vehicular. People and cars must be moved on and off site and around the site for various purposes.

Traffic must enter the site, which brings considerations for the relation to off-site situations. Where are the access streets, and at what points on the site edges can entry be achieved? Do people walk onto the site from somewhere, is there a mass transit connection nearby, or do they primarily enter by vehicles? What is the amount of traffic flow and when does it occur? What is the potential impact of site-related traffic on local streets?

Traffic problems may be relatively simple or may be complicated by various issues. Moving around may be difficult on very tight or small sites with little space outside the building. Moving may be essentially horizontal or may be up and down with multilevel drives or parking. Pedestrian and/or vehicular traffic may be complicated by the many different classes of pedestrians or vehicles, which require different entry points, different forms of traffic paths, separation of traffic, various forms of security control, etc. In addition to building occupants and visitors, consideration must typically be given to access and traffic paths for the fire trucks, trash pickups, and service and delivery vehicles.

In various ways traffic must usually be related to the buildings on a site. Most of the traffic will probably relate to building entry, so entry to the site is only the first stage in the traffic flow. The site plan must be tested for continuous entry and exit paths. The traffic paths must be functionally usable, barrier-free, and continuous in nature for the entire path of travel.

Traffic usually takes place on some form of pavement that is designed to accommodate the specific type of traffic, its form, and its rate of flow. Vehicular traffic must be on continuous, smooth surfaces, generally employing ramps or sloped drives for any vertical movement. Pedestrian traffic may use ramps, but also possibly stairs, elevators, escalators, or other people movers. However, movement of persons with limited abilities must also be accommodated in some manner, either by the basic travel paths or some usable alternatives. The right of access is being increasingly protected by codes and design standards.

In general, design standards for traffic-accommodating elements change over time as new regulations are enacted and enforced or new attitudes emerge about safety and the general optimization for usage. Width of paths, maximum permitted or desirable slopes, the character of surfaces (nonslip, etc.), and other details are typically developed from some combination of legal restrictions, research-generated data, proven experience, personal preference, and outright guesswork.

At present, pedestrian traffic paths are highly restricted in form by the requirements for barrier-free access for use by persons with limited capabilities. These requirements are elements of local building codes, some state codes, and now federal regulations, and they have now become major factors in site design. Planners of site traffic elements for pedestrians should investigate the specific enforceable requirements for a given site.

Facilitation of vehicular traffic must relate to the specific form of vehicles. The range is considerable—from bicycles to large trucks or busses. A major concern is for the required minimum radius of turning, which limits the planning of corners in the traffic paths. Other concerns are for the width of paths, the need to accommodate two-way traffic, and the development of parking.

Figure 4.1 provides some data for the planning of vehicular traffic paths relating primarily to needs for automobiles. Provisions for larger vehicles (fire trucks, etc.) must be developed in relation to each specific vehicle and its activities on the site (access, parking, unloading, long-term storage, etc.).

Figure 4.2 gives information on the planning of site elements for pedestrian travel on sites not requiring barrier-free access. Implementation of these requirements involves some personal judgment, as private property with no commerical use generally does not stipulate the inclusion of barrier-free access.

Figure 4.3 provides data for the planning of site facilities in compliance with current standards for barrier-free access. These requirements generally apply to all public-use facilities and to commerical facilities with more than a certain number of employees or with services to the public. These regulations are subject to ongoing modification and specific local code requirements.

As with any regulations, stipulated requirements with quantified values are

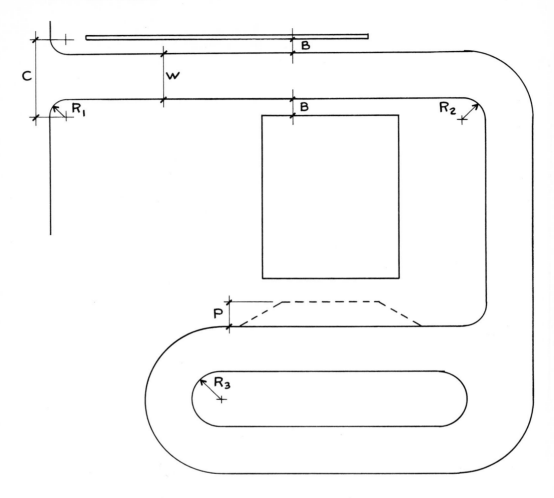

W = Drive width. Depends on vehicle size and whether traffic is
      one-way or two-way. Minimum of 9 ft for one-way, 15 ft for two-way.

R = Radius for turns. Depends on vehicle size and speed of traffic.
      Minimum for cars: R_1 = 6 ft, R_2 = 10 ft, R_3 = 15 ft.

C = Curb cut. Negotiated with owner of street. Depends on proximity
      of other cuts, street corners, etc.

B = Buffer distance. To keep vehicles from hitting objects if they
      stay on the drive. Vehicle overhang requires space beyond curb.
      Creates wider drive space than edge of paving implies. No set
      dimensions; depends on vehicles and protection desired.

P = Pullout. 1.5 times vehicle width to assure clear traffic lane.

FIGURE 4.1 Site layout criteria for automobiles

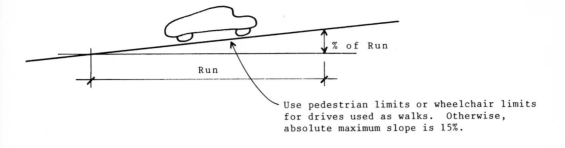

% of Run

Run

Use pedestrian limits or wheelchair limits
for drives used as walks. Otherwise,
absolute maximum slope is 15%.

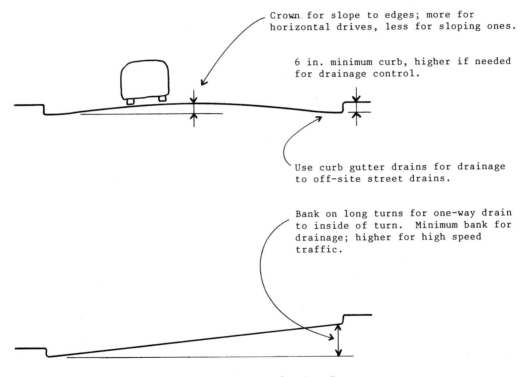

Crown for slope to edges; more for
horizontal drives, less for sloping ones.

6 in. minimum curb, higher if needed
for drainage control.

Use curb gutter drains for drainage
to off-site street drains.

Bank on long turns for one-way drain
to inside of turn. Minimum bank for
drainage; higher for high speed
traffic.

FIGURE 4.1 (*Continued*)

usually minimal, and where something beyond minimal necessity is desired,
designs may be developed with greater generosity.

4.3 PARKING

Accommodation of parking space for vehicles is a frequent requirement for
building sites. Parking may be developed as *surface parking* on paved areas

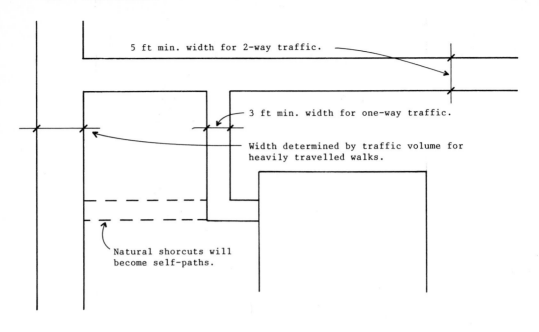

5 ft min. width for 2-way traffic.

3 ft min. width for one-way traffic.

Width determined by traffic volume for heavily travelled walks.

Natural shorcuts will become self-paths.

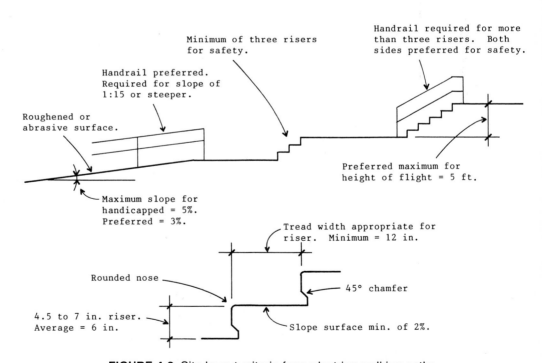

Minimum of three risers for safety.

Handrail required for more than three risers. Both sides preferred for safety.

Handrail preferred. Required for slope of 1:15 or steeper.

Roughened or abrasive surface.

Preferred maximum for height of flight = 5 ft.

Maximum slope for handicapped = 5%. Preferred = 3%.

Tread width appropriate for riser. Minimum = 12 in.

Rounded nose

45° chamfer

4.5 to 7 in. riser. Average = 6 in.

Slope surface min. of 2%.

FIGURE 4.2 Site layout criteria for pedestrian walking paths

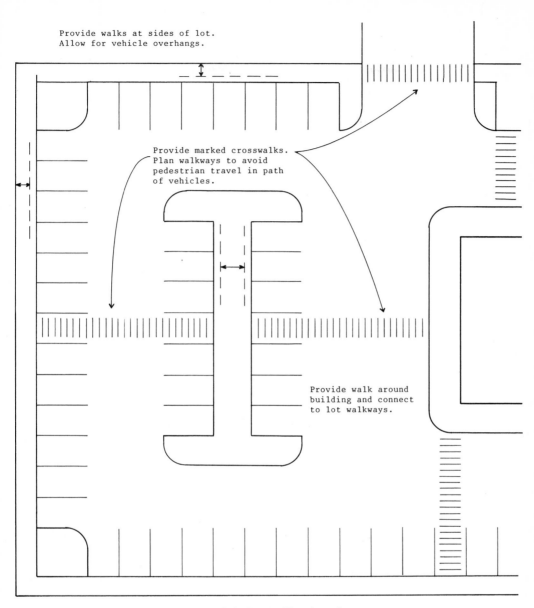

Provide walks at sides of lot.
Allow for vehicle overhangs.

Provide marked crosswalks.
Plan walkways to avoid
pedestrian travel in path
of vehicles.

Provide walk around
building and connect
to lot walkways.

FIGURE 4.2 (*Continued*)

for the site. It can also be developed as *structure parking* in conjunction with the building or in a separate structure on the site. In some cases, all forms of parking may be provided on a single site.

This section deals primarily with surface parking, although the problems of entry and exit for structure parking are also discussed. Parking must be developed in association with general development of traffic accommodations on the site for both vehicular and pedestrian traffic. The vehicles must be able

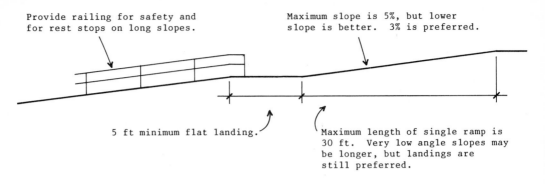

Provide railing for safety and
for rest stops on long slopes.

Maximum slope is 5%, but lower
slope is better. 3% is preferred.

5 ft minimum flat landing.

Maximum length of single ramp is
30 ft. Very low angle slopes may
be longer, but landings are
still preferred.

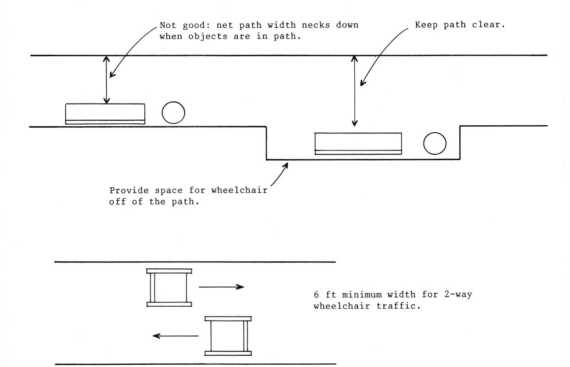

Not good: net path width necks down
when objects are in path.

Keep path clear.

Provide space for wheelchair
off of the path.

6 ft minimum width for 2-way
wheelchair traffic.

FIGURE 4.3 Example criteria for providing barrier-free access on sites. (Specific code criteria should be determined for a particular project.)

to get into and out of the parking, and the people must be able to get back and forth between the parking and the buildings.

The average size of the parking stall has shrunk in recent years as many motorists have opted for "compact" cars instead of the great gas-guzzling land cruisers of the past. Developers of commercial and public parking lots have happily complied by reducing the size of parking stalls, width of drives, radius of corners, and the general acreage of pavement required for a given amount of parking. This is a matter of judgment regarding the accommodation of specific size vehicles, but given that no advocacy group surfaced to assert the rights of motorists with large cars, the era of skimpy parking stalls is probably here to stay.

On the other hand, most parking lots must now have a certain percentage of stalls dedicated to a required number of "handicapped" parking, which requires stalls of almost twice the size of those for compact cars. Access to and from these stalls may also involve some special facilities to accommodate motorists in wheelchairs.

Development of a significant amount of surface parking can eat up enormous amounts of the site area. A rough rule of thumb is that the total area required for a parking lot, with stalls, drive throughs, turn around spaces, and access drives takes from 300 to 350 ft^2 per parked car. Add any significant area for walks, planted divider strips, or the use of low-efficiency criteria in terms of space per vehicle, and the tally goes up.

Figure 4.4 provides some data for the layout of parking lots for passenger automobiles, using minimal criteria for stall sizes, drive widths, and turning radiuses. This criteria provides for quite tight parking and driving, and a more commodious facility will require increases in all the dimensions.

Figure 4.5 provides some criteria for the layout of parking for qualified handicapped persons. Basic concerns here are the ability to open a car door fully and accommodation of a wheelchair between cars. In addition, there must be a barrier-free path to and from the parking space, which may affect the use of curbs in the parking lot.

Vast acres of parked cars are a familiar American landscape feature, but generally not a very attractive one. Where some enhancement of appearance is desired, a number of techniques can be used to relieve the sterile paved surface of the empty lot as well as the clutter of the full lot. Views of lots may be screened from viewing positions off the site by surrounding the lots with walls or rows or trees of high shrubs. Lots may be broken up into several small lots instead of one giant one, and possibly scattered around the site with some distance between lots.

Large parking lots, or any lot, can be made more attractive by placing some landscaping elements inside the lot—plantings, banked earth forms, large rocks, site scupture, decorative lighting, etc. Where the site form can be altered, some vertical differences in levels may be achieved, relieving an endless, flat monotony of continuous surfacing.

In general, getting back and forth from the parking lot to the building should be made as easy, safe, and pleasant as possible. Walking to and from cars can be made safer with walks that are separate from the driving lanes. Covering or enclosing the walking paths can make the travel better during inclement weather. For night use, good general lighting will significantly improve the security in the lot.

Signage, traffic controls, and special security elements such as key-oper-

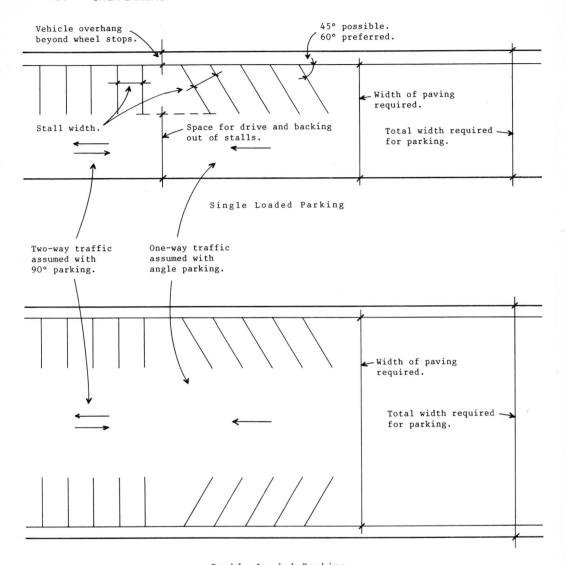

Vehicle overhang
beyond wheel stops.

45° possible.
60° preferred.

Stall width.

Space for drive and backing
out of stalls.

Width of paving
required.

Total width required
for parking.

Single Loaded Parking

Two-way traffic
assumed with
90° parking.

One-way traffic
assumed with
angle parking.

Width of paving
required.

Total width required
for parking.

Double Loaded Parking

FIGURE 4.4 Layout data for parking for automobiles

ated gates are sometimes required for parking. Separation of users may require separate lots, different points of vehicular entry, different pedestrian access paths, etc.

Zoning requirements often stipulate a minimum number of parking spaces for various building occupancies. Satisfying these or other criteria for total required parking can often generate a considerable assignment of space of parking for a project. This often becomes a major site planning issue and one

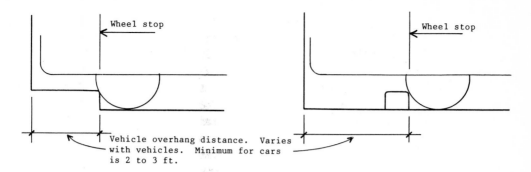

Wheel stop

Wheel stop

Vehicle overhang distance. Varies
with vehicles. Minimum for cars
is 2 to 3 ft.

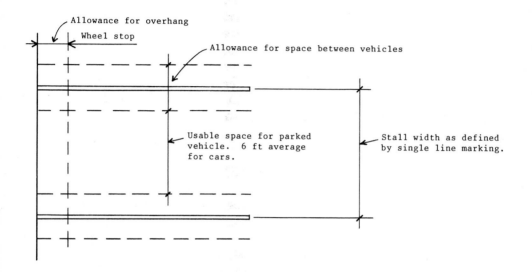

Allowance for overhang

Wheel stop

Allowance for space between vehicles

Usable space for parked
vehicle. 6 ft average
for cars.

Stall width as defined
by single line marking.

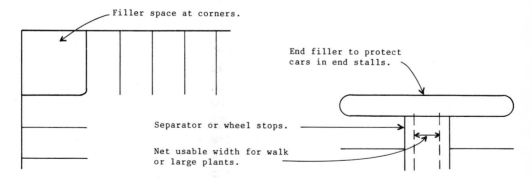

Filler space at corners.

End filler to protect
cars in end stalls.

Separator or wheel stops.

Net usable width for walk
or large plants.

FIGURE 4.4 (*Continued*)

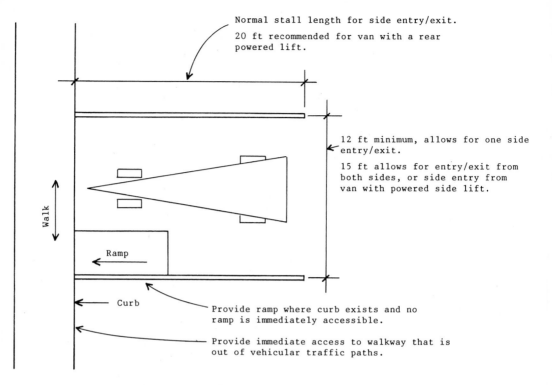

Normal stall length for side entry/exit.
20 ft recommended for van with a rear powered lift.

12 ft minimum, allows for one side entry/exit.

15 ft allows for entry/exit from both sides, or side entry from van with powered side lift.

Walk

Ramp

Curb

Provide ramp where curb exists and no ramp is immediately accessible.

Provide immediate access to walkway that is out of vehicular traffic paths.

FIGURE 4.5 Example criteria for handicapped parking. (Specific code criteria should be determined for a particular project.)

that may establish limits for the use of the property in general for a specific occupancy. The efficient design of parking, with minimal criteria, becomes a major issue for many sites.

4.4   THE VISIBLE SITE

Site planning most notably deals with the visible portions of the site: what is seen, walked on, and generally participated in by the users of the site and the buildings on it. The viewing of the visible site, its construction, use, and relations to the surrounding environment are the major aspects of the design work for site planning.

While activities may occur out of view on the inside of a building, whatever happens on the site is generally accessible to viewing—a public event often shared by occupants of the building and persons off the site, as well as those on the site at any given time.

From an aesthetic point of reference, the viewing of the site is as important to the site designer as the appearance of the building exterior is to the architect. In the end, of course, both the site and the building exterior are parts of the same landscape and "viewing" generally encompasses them both.

Designing for the viewing of sites is complicated by the fact that it does not occur as a singular act, but in many different situations. Various possible viewing situations for the designer to consider include the following:

Viewing from all possible points: on the site, off the site, from inside the building, from neighboring buildings, etc.

Viewing at night, during daylight, with site lighting turned on or off

Viewing at different times of the year, as the seasons affect the landscape and environment of the site

Viewing by persions in vehicles, driving past or onto the site; viewing by persons walking

Viewing may be studied essentially for its pleasurable effects, or relate to some functional concerns, such as the ability to locate building entrances, find entry to parking lots, see and avoid collisions with cross traffic, and so on. Where heavy security is required, viewing may be critical and obscuring of the view of any part of the site may be objectionable.

Viewing of the site may be a major concern in dealing with persons who own or use surrounding properties. The undeveloped site may have been attractive to them, and the design for the developed site may be inherently a potential eyesore in their opinions; hence the need for major attention to the view from off the site.

On the other hand, attractive development of a formerly ugly-appearing site may help to offset objections about the development of the property. The overall improvement of the neighborhood appearance may enhance the value of other properties; maybe only aesthetically, but quite possibly also in actual dollar value.

Somewhere in the myriad of pragmatic problems to be solved in site planning, it is to be hoped that the nature of the viewed, visible site is always given considerable attention.

4.5 THE INVISIBLE SITE

There is also the invisible site—that is, what is not in view because it is underground. If nothing else, this consists of the geological formation underlying the site surface. At a minimum, the development of the surface and any plantings or construction on it must relate to the subsurface ground conditions.

The inventory of existing site materials must be left in place, utilized for reconstruction, or removed. The need for or the feasibility of doing this work may influence some planning decisions. Raising or lowering of the finished grade of the site or achieving some special form must be considered in pragmatic terms that involve considerations for the below-grade soil materials and geological structure.

For most building sites there will also be various constructed elements beneath the site surface. Piping and wiring for building services may enter the site and the building underground. Installations may also require access manholes, tunnels, underground vaults, and other buried elements. Items such as fuel tanks, surface mounted equipment, and underground vaults must be located to provide access for service. These items can present major problems in terms of their relation to development of site planting or construction.

When placed at significant depths, underground construction can involve considerable excavation and the site surface may need to be developed over great depths of backfill. Assuring the integrity of the finished site surface may be a challenge in this situation. Especially affected will be pavements and small constructions for curbs, planters, and short walls, which will most likely have shallow footing in the site surface. The integrity of backfill as a base for surface construction is often difficult to ensure. Planning may avoid major problems in this regard, but careful detailing of the construction to tolerate some minor movements may be more important.

An underground activity that goes on through the life of the site is the nurturing of plantings; often involving considerable irrigation and the development of extensive root systems. These problems are discussed elsewhere in this book, but an important planning concern is the locating of trees and large shrubs and any plantings that need major amounts of continuous irrigation. Where these have potential for disastrous effects, their locations (or possibly their choice in the first place) need careful consideration.

Just as the site surface is a shared space—with buildings, drives, walks, plantings, site constructions, and parking lots—so is the underground space—with tree roots, buried piping and wiring, foundations, vaults, buried tanks, and various possible elements. The space below needs as much planning as the surface space. And, of course, the surface and subsurface spaces are directly linked and related, making the planning a singular effort.

4.6 MANAGEMENT OF SITE MATERIALS

An existing site represents an inventory of materials. Decisions must be made that involve the management of this inventory in the process of developing the site. These decisions may entail the removal, rearrangement, modification, or replacement of materials. The nature of the existing site and the type of redevelopment will determine the extent to which site modification is required.

Site Materials

Site materials can be broadly divided between those below grade and those above. Below grade are mostly various soil, rock, and water deposits. For previously developed sites there may also be various below-grade constructions. For heavily forested sites, there may be considerable root growth below grade.

Trees or other plant growth may be above the ground surface. Preservation or removal of these must be determined in conjunction with the site development plans, which is discussed in Chapter 7. If preservation is desired, it may be necessary to develop careful plans to protect existing growth during site work and construction. Raising or lowering the grade, major changes in surface drainage, and other modifications may seriously affect existing growth.

General concerns for soil materials are discussed in Appendix A, which also describes various soil properties and the means of identifying soil types. Soil is basically natural, but modifications are possible, and indeed often necessary, for site development.

In general, existing site materials must be viewed as a given inventory of materials to be managed in the site development process. The existing materials may be removed, replaced, modified, relocated on the site, or simply be left as is and protected.

Problems that might affect the management of site materials include the following.

Establishment of Finished Grades. If the level of the site surface (grade) is to be substantially raised or lowered, there will be a major need for removal or importation of materials.

Building Excavation. For large buildings with extensive below-grade construction, the excavation for construction may involve extensive removal of site materials. These may be used elsewhere on the site or require considerable planning for transportation and disposal off site.

Extensive Landscaping. Where existing topsoil is lacking or inadequate, major new plantings may require the importation of considerable material for surface soils to sustain plant growth.

Site Construction. Extensive development of site structures may require removal of soils displaced by the construction.

Some special problems involving these and other concerns are discussed in the next section of this chapter. The anticipation of these problems will often affect the type and extent of data required from site surveys and subsurface investigations, as discussed in Chapter 3.

Removal of Soil

Where possible, the ideal situation is that of balancing the cuts and fills required to achieve finished grades so that no significant removal or importing of soils is required. However, this is not always possible, and major removal may sometimes be required.

A common situation requiring extensive removal of soil is that of major below-grade construction. Most sites are not raised or lowered significantly, simply because they must retain some connection to the site boundary conditions of neighboring properties or streets. Site construction therefore displaces soils that must be removed.

The other major reason for removal of existing site materials is that they are undesirable for some reason. For plantings, better support of pavements, drainage, or for other reasons, the existing soils may be unusable and not feasibly modifiable.

Removed soils must be taken somewhere, which presents another problem to be solved in the site development; the more so if the soil materials are of types that are for some reason undesirable.

Imported Materials

In the best of situations, the materials desired for importing to one site may be those required to be removed from another site. Where extensive, ongoing construction occurs, this exchange is frequently made.

Topsoil for plantings required for one site may be removed from another site that is to be covered mostly with buildings, site constructions, and pavements. Or, the soil removed to achieve a major excavation on one site may be used to raise a major depressed portion of another site.

Where this is not the case, the practicality of a particular proposed site development may hinge on the feasibility of obtaining the necessary imported soil materials.

Modification of Site Materials

Existing site materials often represent usable raw materials that require some modification for the purposes of the site development. Surface soils to be reused for finish grading may need to be cleaned of debris, large roots, rocks, and so on. Soils to be used for structural purposes, such as base supports for pavements or as bearing supports for foundations, generally need compaction and occasionally some other forms of modification. These latter modifications may improve soil strength, resistance to settlement-producing deformations, or general soil stability, or they may change water-related properties.

Various forms of soil modification and the means of achieving them are discussed in Section A6 of Appendix A. Feasibility of modifications should be carefully studied before decisions are made regarding major removal or replacement of site materials.

5

BUILDING/SITE RELATIONS

Building sites must obviously be closely related to the buildings that will occupy the site. In many situations the buildings are predominant, and the site is just where the buildings happen to be located. At the other extreme are sites with no buildings at all, or ones that are simply more significant than the buildings on them, such as the sites of major historic events. We assert a democratic attitude here, stating that the buildings are important, but so is the site. Thus, by ''relations'' we imply some give and take between the site and the buildings. The buildings are expected to respond to some site concerns, and the site has a significant requirement to accommodate the buildings. It is definitely a two-way relationship.

5.1 SITING THE BUILDING

Establishing the specific geometric, spatial relationship between a building and its site is described as *siting* the building. This generally consists of the following principal considerations.

Horizontal Positioning

Using the general architectural term for a horizontal plane section drawing, horizontal positioning establishes the *plan* location of the building on the site.

Determining the dimensions of this positioning may involve several concerns, including the following (see Figure 5.1).

Requirements for setbacks from property lines

Protection of easements, usually along a side of the property

Allowance of site space for driveways, walks, undergound utilities, etc.

Protection of views or privacy

Allowance for site construction (stairs, retaining walls, etc.) or installation of large trees

Positioning of the building on the site plan may be severely constrained when the site is small in comparison to the building's ground level footprint. In some cases it is possible that the building may actually occupy the total buildable portion of the site—that is, the space on the site not reserved for setbacks, easements, or other restrictions against construction. This can result in virtually no remaining site space, and the site literally *is* the building's ground floor level.

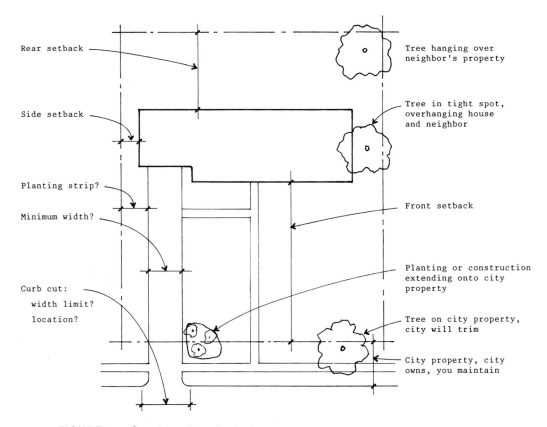

FIGURE 5.1 Considerations for horizontal positioning of buildings on their sites

Obviously the relations between the site and the buildings must begin with consideration of how much of the site is actually required to be developed outside the building. If there is almost no site left, the buildings must generally conform very closely to the plan shape and size of the site. If a good deal of site remains, there is a major amount of site to deal with in design terms, and the buildings are considerably free of plan constraints related to the shape of the site boundaries.

Developing the horizontal layouts of the buildings and their site must be done cooperatively. Many items relate only to the site (the marking of a single parking stall in a lot) and others only to the building (locations of vertical air ducts), but many are of mutual concern. Special purpose buildings have specific size and shape requirements (for a basketball court, for example) and so do certain site features, notably driveways and parking lots. An early analysis to be made in determining site and building plans is that of the various relatively inflexible space requirements for both the site and the buildings.

Vertical Positioning

Vertical location of buildings with respect to their sites is often a difficult design decision. There are many potential relationships for a building in this regard, including the following (see Figure 5.2):

Relation to existing streets that provide access to the site

Relation to any existing buildings or other features that have a determined location and some relationship to the building being positioned

Relation to existing site features, such as existing grades, elements to be preserved, ground water levels, soil conditions for foundations, etc.

Relation to existing underground utilities, especially sewer mains that use gravity flow

Obviously, establishing the finished site form and the elevations for site elements will be closely related to the vertical position of the building. This

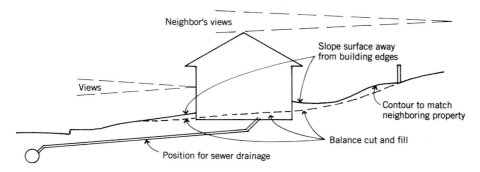

FIGURE 5.2 Considerations for vertical positioning of buildings on their sites

may involve matters such as the feasible slope for drives or pedestrian ramps, or the development of site drainage.

In addition to practical and technical concerns, there are various design considerations regarding the view of the building on the site, views from inside the building, and the overall landscape and building designs.

5.2 THE BUILDING BASE

The most intimate contact between a building and its site occurs at the base of the building. The site itself is a major part of the building base. For architectural design purposes, it is desirable to express this and to develop both the building and site in a very close relationship.

One important aspect of this relationship is that between the general site plan and the entry level plan of the building. This may be simple for a small building on a flat site, but it can also be quite complex for large buildings with many entry points or sites with many levels.

The building may "sit" on a site in various ways. The general problems of its horizontal and vertical positioning are discussed in the preceding section. Figure 5.3 shows a range of possibilities for the general placement of a building on a site, dealing primarily with its vertical position with respect to the ground plane. This ranges from a fully underground building to one that is virtually suspended in midair.

While buildings do indeed exist in all of the situations illustrated in Figure 5.3, by far the most common forms are those shown in Figure 5.3c and d. Figure 5.3c represents the building with some basement space, while Figure 5.3d depicts the building without a basement. Basements, and indeed fully underground spaces, require special considerations for many details of the construction. These become more critical if the below-grade spaces are occupied for other than utilitarian purposes—that is, for other than storage, parking, or housing of equipment.

In order to open up site-level space in some situations, it is sometimes possible to extend basement spaces outside the building, literally developing some fully underground spaces. This necessitates some site surface develop-

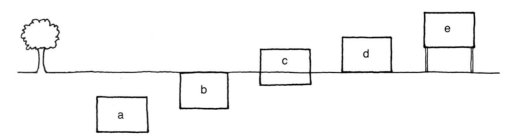

FIGURE 5.3 Building/ground relationships with respect to the ground surface plane

ment that is literally on top of the roof of the underground spaces. Some of the implications and details of this construction are presented in Section 8.8.

An important part of the building base is that which constitutes the building foundation. Choice of the general form of foundation and the work necessary for its installation must be closely coordinated with other aspects of the site work. The need to extensively excavate for basements or foundations requires study of the disposition of the excavated materials and the ensuing problems of developing site surfaces with extensive backfill (refilling of the excessive excavation).

Many building services enter or exit the building at its base, often below the site finished grade. Sewer, water supply, and gas supply piping is usually here. Where electrical power and communication lines are underground, they may also enter in this manner. The services warrant consideration in the development of site construction and can affect the positioning of the building on the site. This is discussed more fully in Section 5.4.

5.3 ACCESS

An important function for building sites is accommodating access to the building. The access path typically begins with concern for access onto the site, which is usually constrained by adjacent properties or streets. Access here refers generally to two forms of traffic: pedestrian and vehicular. Where different groups of people and/or vechicles are involved, it may be quite complex.

Initial access onto a site typically involves the use of public thoroughfares. If curbs, gutters, and sidewalks exist at the edges of these streets, some disruption and reconstruction is usually required. The limits and specific construction details for this work must be negotiated with local authorities.

For large sites, or those involving large volumes of traffic, the use of existing streets may require environmental impact reports and traffic studies. Modifications or improvements of existing streets or traffic controls may be necessary, and impact of noise on neighborhoods may be critical. This may affect decisions regarding where and how access to the site is established.

An important factor in accessibility is that regarding persons with limited abilities. This may involve persons in wheelchairs, but can also refer to the very old, the very young, the vision-impaired, or those who cannot read words on signs. General concerns for barrier-free sites are discussed in Section 9.5.

Access in most cases is controlled in some way. This may consist of the placement of walks or drives and the location of entry doors for buildings. It can be more firmly controlled by the use of fences, walls, and gates. For highly secured facilities, such as prisons or military installations, controlled access is a major factor.

For the average building and site, the general intent is to *facilitate* access as much as possible. Buildings can be either inviting or formidable in this regard. A major site design goal is often that of making the passage onto and through the site a pleasurable experience. Planning, structuring, and landscaping of the site all work toward this goal.

5.4   BUILDING SERVICES

Buildings must typically be linked to a variety of external services. Common ones include the following:

Water supply
Sewers—possibly two: one for sanitary waste and one for storm water
Electrical power
Gas
Telephone lines
Cable TV
Mail delivery, on a regular basis with some specific drop point
General delivery: mail, newspapers, UPS, etc. (often with vehicles)
Trash collection; often involving some regular site storage or pickup point
Firefighting

All of these generally require some facilitation on or passage through the site. The location of the building on the site and specific entry points to the building will affect placement of these items. However, they must also be linked to some locations *off* the site: to streets, existing utility mains, etc. Various details regarding existing streets and utilities will often establish some considerable number of fixed references for the building/site interaction.

Of particular concern for site design is the need for relatively inflexible locations for these service elements. Early identification of the specific services required for a building and site and the existence (if any) of fixed sources is important. Bringing water, electric, gas, and telephone lines to a site is usually constrained to some degree by the existence of general services already in place and the standard means for tapping into them.

A particularly critical concern is access to sewer systems. A principal consideration is their location. An issue in this regard is at what vertical elevation the delivery of wastes must be made to the sewer mains. Wastes are essentially water-borne and flow by gravity; if the building is a long distance from the sewer, or is not considerably above it, this can be a problem. Pumping of sewage to a higher level to facilitate its drainage is possible, but it is an expensive and maintenance-intensive alternative.

Specific elements required for other services depend in most cases on the size of the operation on the site. The items involved in delivering electricity to a small house are quite different than those required for a large shopping center or tall office building. Certain basic elements are required in any case, but their size, location, and accessibility may be considerably different.

Many service elements are placed underground, and their existence may not greatly affect the surface development of the site. They must, however, be integrated into the general site development, especially where considerable site construction is planned.

Of greater concern, however, are elements that must be placed on the site surface or connected to it. This may include items such as the following.

Trash dumps for regular pickup

Manholes to underground installations

Fire hydrants

Mail boxes

Telephone booths

Public street lighting

Traffic signs

Electrical transformers and meters

Water and gas shutoffs and meters

Poles or towers for overhead transmission of power, phone, or cable TV lines

Curbside and area drains to storm sewers

Like it or not, these elements will become part of the landscape. They must be incorporated in a way that recognizes their usage and requirements. This is often a major challenge with a site for which an attractive appearance is a goal. It is necessary first to establish their exact requirements and the degree to which flexibility of location or form is possible. Then it may be possible to consider their potential uses for other site purposes.

A major consideration for any complex construction project is that of construction sequences. It is important to recognize this in considering what effects it may have on design and the general development of design plans and specifications. Especially vulnerable in this regard is the finish work for the site surface development. Topping materials for finish grading, planting installations, and general site construction work should not be disrupted by work on underground construction performed out of sequence.

5.5 BUILDING/SITE SPATIAL CONTINUITY

In the best of design situations, the building and its site are considered as a connected and continuous spatial entity. Thus the design of each is not fully

FIGURE 5.4 Connected site spaces developed with some sympathy from the architect of the buildings and a desire to make pedestrian passage interesting

separated, but rather continuously linked. This involves the following major concerns (see Figure 5.4):

Recognition of the externally viewed building as an object on the site, fusing in a visual sense with everything else on the site, as well as with what is viewed generally in the scope of vision of the viewer extending as far as the eye can see.

Recognition of what is seen from inside the building: by whom, in what manner, and for what duration—again, with the whole scope of vision considered.

Recognition that entry and exit passages are a continuous, sequential experience, including involvements off the site, on the site, and inside the building. This passage should have a smooth functional nature, but should also, hopefully, be a stimulating and pleasant experience.

The designed experience here is one that involves people moving, usually on foot or in vehicles. This is an experience hard to visualize and harder to demonstrate convincingly to others. Still, it is the ultimate test of the work; not how it looks in drawings, small scale models, or photographs of the finished work, but how it is *personally experienced.*

Probably the only reasonably convincing explanation of a proposed design in this regard is by analogy with some existing situation. With understood limitations in terms of context, this can be very useful to both the designer and the potential users. Caution should be made as to the relative impossibility of exact duplication, but the general form and/or feel of a real space, experienced at full scale, is hard to beat when used in combination with other more conventional means to explain design work.

5.6 THE BUILDING MODIFIED BY THE SITE

Buildings must establish some degree of compatibility with their sites. This is an interactive relationship with certain undeniably fundamental and functional aspects. Hopefully it is a relationship of mutual respect. (See Fig. 5.5.)

Some sites may be truly hostile or unusable: old swamps, former dump sites, reclaimed areas ravaged by industrial pollution or exploitation, and so on. It may be necessary to virtually create a whole new site from a design point of view to maximize the accommodation of the building.

However, the typical site has a considerable number of features that any building designed for it must relate to; or at least ought to for good design. It is this typical situation that is considered in the following discussion.

Functional Requirements

Some things are virtually unavoidable. Some major considerations of this nature are as follows.

The building foundations must be developed in terms of the true existing conditions of the site, regarding subsurface ground materials, ground water levels, seismicity, potential instabilities, etc.

FIGURE 5.5 Building group, sited to express its hillside involvement

The building's vertical positioning must be established in terms of site conditions with regard to feasible development of the finished site surfaces as it affects building entry, views from the building interior, etc.

The building's horizontal positioning, general compass orientation, and possibly actual horizontal shape (plan profile) must relate to the site boundary form and dimensions.

In purely functional terms, it is important to establish very early what is fixed and what can be manipulated or negotiated during the design.

General Compatibility

Beyond more functional adequacy is the concept of a truly symbiotic relationship between the building and its site. This refers to a more complex definition of the role of the site and its relative importance to the building design.

Many of these issues are, of course, not limited to the building/site relationship, but extend to the conditions at and beyond the site edges. In many situations they extend to the entire viewed perimeter and include situations regarding adjacent properties, nearby buildings, and possibly the community or neighborhood as a whole. The importance of these relations may be largely up to the personal attitudes of the designer or building owners, but in some situations may actually be controlled by local zoning, building codes, or prior negotiated property right restrictions.

It should be established early in the design process just what is *required* in these regards and what is a matter of the design goals or attitudes of the designer and owner. The basic idea is to develop the building design as a realistic and compatible concept in view of the true site conditions. In this reference, "site" includes the actual property of the owner and the extended environment.

5.7   THE SITE MODIFIED BY THE BUILDING

Of course, sites are modified immensely by the presence of a building. We intend to discuss here some issues that affect the basic concepts driving the design work for a site development in specific response to building design issues.

The site for a building must be transformed in two primary ways (see Figure 5.6).

It must give up some portion of its space to the building, in effect, accepting the building as a new site object to be accommodated by the remaining site spaces.

FIGURE 5.6 Site requiring an unavoidable flattening of a nonflat condition. This requires an extreme, but functionally necessary intrusion on the natural site.

It must perform a major new function: that of accommodating access and exit paths for the building, including the building users and all building services. It may also be necessary for some or all remaining site spaces to be developed as accessory to the building (walks, drives, terraces, storage, etc.).

In these regards, there is literally no such thing as an *undisturbed site*, if it must accommodate a building. Any undisturbed character refers only to the portions of the site not actually occupied by or used for access to the building. For a large site, this may be a lot of space; for tight, urban sites, it is often little or none.

Major modifications of sites occur when the finished site surface must be substantially raised or lowered from its original location, or when hilly sites must be flattened out; flat ones given some major sculptural form. The original site may actually disappear, and the site design consists of virtually creating a whole new site.

The whole character of what constitutes a site design effort is often strongly influenced by the extent to which the proposed building project calls for modification of the site. The only remnants of the original site in many cases occur at the site edges, where boundary conditions are limited in terms of change.

6

DEVELOPING THE SITE FORM

A major part of site design involves the general shaping of the contoured form of the site surface. The surface, of course, includes that portion occupied by the building. However, we are referring here primarily to the site surface outside the building. This area may become somewhat obscured when the building and site are considerably blended, with interior courts, decks, covered outdoor spaces, etc. Nevertheless, the discussions in this chapter deal essentially with the site's outdoor spaces.

6.1 MODIFICATION OF THE SITE FORM

In some situations it may be desirable to preserve as much of the site as possible in its original form. This is a special "design" problem of its own, later discussed in Section 7.3. In most cases, however, it is necessary to modify considerably the site, in addition to erecting a building on it.

The simple geometry of the site form relates to many design concerns. It also presents many potential technical problems in terms of achieving a desired form and assuring its stability over time under the ravages of weather and usage. Judgments about modifications of the site form must be made in the context of both of these considerations: relations to site functions and problems of achieving and preserving the desired form. The remaining sections of this chapter deal with various major issues of both these concerns.

6.2 CUT AND FILL

A basic process involved in modifying the surface profile of a site is that of
cut and fill. Simply put, cutting is the removal of some of the existing surface
and filling is building up of the surface. However, the true end result is basically the redefinition of the surface, involving a comparison of the before
(original site) and after (finished, new surface).

To develop the new site surface it is necessary to begin with a complete
definition of existing conditions. This includes a precise analysis of the geometry (shape) of the surface, an inventory of objects on the surface (trees,
rock outcroppings, streams, etc.), and some investigation of the immediate
subsurface materials. This total package of information is typically assembled
with the site survey (map with horizontal and vertical dimensions), a geotechnical survey (soil borings and report), and some site inspection (recorded
with photographs and notes).

One early design decision involves the potential use of existing surface
materials. This may result in the preservation of materials and objects (topsoil, specimen trees, interesting ground forms, etc.). Early site plans may
incorporate these elements and establish some reference points for the overall
site development. This can range from an almost fully preserved site to one
that is totally cleared and reconstructed, depending on both existing conditions
and design goals.

Some basic concerns of managing the existing site materials are discussed
in Section 4.8. The issue being considered here is the process of cut and fill.
In its simplest terms, this may merely consist of rearranging the site surface
materials into a different surface contour, as shown in Figure 6.1. A basic
goal is often that of balancing the cut and fill volumes in order to minimize
the necessity to either remove them from the site or import to the site any
considerable volume of soil materials.

However, it is seldom that simple. Some site surface materials are either
undesirable (junk, wrong soil type, etc.) or more suitable for use elsewhere
on the site. Thus, an initial cut may be made to remove these materials to
produce a specially prepared site surface on which the new surface will be
filled.

Finished surfaces that are essentially cut down are different in character
from those that are considerably built up with fill. Cutting down a significant
amount means exposing subsurface materials, which may involve some geotechnical problems. This must be thoroughly studied by a soils analyst or other
knowledgeable professional who has the results of any exploratory subsurface
investigations.

Filling a significant amount, on the other hand, presents the problem of
stabilizing the finished surface. Some settlement of the finished surface is
inevitable as the man-made soil deposits coalesce by various processes to
achieve a comfortable arrangement; the principal factors being gravity, water,

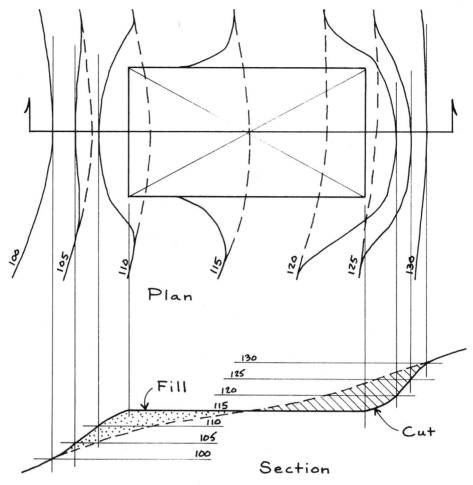

FIGURE 6.1 Cuts and fills

earthquake vibrations, and any natural time-dependent deformation responses of the soils.

Stabilizing filled surfaces is a major construction problem. It becomes more critical in certain soils or climate conditions, with an increase in the depth of fill, and when some surface construction is involved. For practical purposes, it is best to avoid excessive filling if possible. The costs are generally considerable to achieve the fill, ensure its stability, and design surface construction to work on top of it. There may be no alternative in some situations, but the cost and effort to make it work well should be understood.

6.3   GRADING

Grading is a construction process that recontours the ground surface. This involves sculpting the surface materials to a newly defined profile and typically requires cutting and/or filling. As it is a multistage process, it requires more than simply attaining a new dimension.

The first step is a preliminary grading to obtain a base for initial construction. This also often strips off either undesirable materials or those being preserved for later use. This step precedes the excavation for building foundations and major site constructions.

As construction proceeds, the grade (site surface definition) may be progressively developed. Excavated materials may be used as general surface fill, or merely as backfill (refilling the excess excavation required to perform construction). Eventually, the site surface will be covered with some combination of buildings, pavements and other site constructions, and some open ground surfaces that may sustain cultivated or existing plantings.

The *finished grade* is thus actually defined by the combination of structures and ground surfaces. Where the site has considerable construction, there may be little or even no open ground. The soil surfaces may simply consist of minor infilling between the construction elements, in which case the construction will basically perform the essential task of the grading.

At the other extreme is the almost fully preserved site, which requires minimum excavation and construction. The finished grade *is* virtually the original site in this case.

The more typical case is some final surface soil definition developed as part of the final landscaping work. This may require some general surface grading work, followed by trimming up and installing plant-sustaining topsoil, plantings, and decorative elements.

6.4 DRAINAGE

A major factor to be dealt with in the development of the site surface form is water drainage from the surface. This entails a significant consideration for water from precipitation (rain and melting ice or snow), as well as runoff from possible excessive irrigation.

In some situations, drainage may relate only to site surface form considerations, but the more typical case also requires considerations for most of the following:

Protection from erosion of surface materials (principally soil in sloped planted areas)

Protection of site construction from water effects: pressures of saturated soils, washouts of supporting soils, etc.

Disposition of the drained water: collection, channelling, delivery to sewers, etc.

Protection of neighboring properties from runoff water caused by changes in site conditions

Solving any drainage "problems" must take into account all aspects of drainage as a whole. However, the formation of the drainage itself begins with consideration of the site surface geometry since water will basically move by gravity flow. Therefore, an early investigation should be performed to assess the principal factors of water drainage—the pattern of drainage (where the water actually *goes*), the amount of water flow, and the velocity of the flow for the maximum design precipitation rate based on local weather history.

The amount of water flowing has mostly to do with the size of the area on which precipitation falls, the rate of precipitation (intensity of rainfall in inches of surface water per hour), and the rate at which it drains from the watershed area. The latter is influenced by the angle of slope of the area surface and the general surface texture and relative absorption.

Individual portions of the site surface must be investigated using flow rate values based on the surface materials: soil, concrete paving, etc. Water from a light rain or from melting snow will soak into bare soil or a planted surface. However, a heavy rain, which is generally the crux of the design problem, will flow off of any surface that is not dead flat.

Water from building roofs may also form part of the total watershed for a site, unless roof drains feed into a piped storm drain sewer system. Roofs that drain onto the site must be carefully considered for any heavy concentrations of runoff that can wash out site surface materials or elements.

A major problem with drainage is retaining the soils on the site surfaces that are not covered by construction. Plantings with firmly established roots and edging with hard materials may reduce this, but steeply sloped surfaces must be carefully analyzed in this regard. Use of geotextiles or other methods may be employed in the initial construction of the site to protect vulnerable surfaces until plants are well rooted.

Site construction generally plays some role in the control or general management of drainage. (See Figure 6.2.) If nothing else, it affects the site form and, in the case of pavements, the absorptive character of the surface. In most cases, however, construction offers major opportunities for drainage management in terms of collection or channelling.

Paved areas are ordinarily sloped or crowned to promote drainage off the paved surface. However, they can also be used as drainage collectors or channels. Streets and drives with high curbs often have edge gutters that serve a drainage channelling function. Large paved areas often have area drains that feed to a storm drain system: an underground, piped sewer system.

Drainage of a single site must also be viewed in terms of the larger patterns of drainage. What may be an ideal means for handling drainage for a single site may not be reasonable in this regard. A hillside site usually has both uphill and downhill neighbors. Maintaining goodwill, if not actual legal constraints, will affect the management of drainage in this situation.

If not fed directly to a sewer, surface drainage from small sites is often dumped onto streets. This condition must be analyzed to determine the affect

(a)

(b)

FIGURE 6.2 Elements for achieving site surface drainage control.

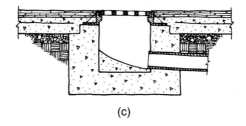

(c)

(d)

FIGURE 6.2 (Continued)

on the streets and any channelled drainage (usually by curb gutters). Also of concern here is the potential for eroded materials being washed onto the streets.

In general, site drainage is both a problem for the site itself and a major factor for the entire site boundary condition. Typically, site development results in increased flow of drainage off the site due to the addition of site areas covered by buildings and pavements. Thus, the existing conditions for both the site and the surrounding areas are inevitably altered.

6.5 SITE EDGE CONSTRAINTS

The many concerns of relating a site to its surroundings are covered in depth throughout this book. However, the primary focus is only those concerns directly involving the site form.

Unless the site is part of a whole, larger area development, the form conditions at the site edges often represent fixed conditions. Freedom to manipulate the form of neighboring properties or bordering streets is highly unlikely. The general scenario is keeping the edges as is and manipulating the form only within the site boundaries.

Even in the situation just described, the edges represent additional constraints. A major one is site drainage to the edges, as discussed in the preceding section. Others may involve limiting access of breezes or sunlight, blocking views, undermining adjacent construction or site surfaces, or creating unpleasant views such as the ugly rear of a building, a trash dump, a parking lot, and so on.

Edges may, in some cases, be built up or cut down through the use of property line retaining walls. Use of any construction on the property edge, even a simple fence, is usually restricted by building codes or other regulations. Major installations here must be negotiated with both neighbors and the local authorities.

As discussed extensively in Chapter 7, major plantings at site edges should be developed with the neighbors' concerns in mind. Blocking views, breezes, or sunlight or creating overhanging growth with various droppings onto the neighboring site surfaces will undermine the potential for goodwill with the neighbors.

Site edge conditions may also affect the general site form development and building placement on the site. A desire to attain prominence, obscurity, or simply some general blending into the neighborhood can be considered in this regard. This may involve the whole site, or simply the view in selected directions. The site boundaries are typically not all the same—it may be desirable in a situation to be prominently viewed from one side (the street), virtually invisible from others (giving both you and the neighbors maximum privacy), and have a general sense of fitting into the overall form and texture of the neighborhood. (See the case study example in Section 10.1.)

6.6 CONTROLLING THE SITE FORM

Development of site form is much more than an exercise in geometry or sculpture. The actual creation and execution of complex or extreme forms can result in major construction problems. This may warrant construction with soil materials alone, but also typically involves some constructed objects, including the base of the building.

The general problems of construction with soils are discussed in Section 8.1. A major form concern is the creation of steeply sloped soil surfaces. Some basic soil structural behaviors must be dealt with in this case, but the overall problem also implies concern for erosion due to precipitation or irrigation. Various measures can be taken to both create and preserve soil profiles, including the use of deeply rooted plantings and various forms of site construction.

Controlling the site form is a major technical issue in site design, and there is no shortcut in fully understanding the potentials and limitations of all the factors involved. The character of soils in terms of basic properties and ordinary structural behaviors is discussed in Appendix A. Many of the problems in using plantings are discussed in Chapter 7. Use of various forms of site construction are discussed in Chapter 8. And, the general interactions of the building and the site are discussed in Chapter 5.

Putting it all together in some real situations is presented in the form of several case studies in Chapter 9. It must be kept in mind that sites exist in a dynamic state, strongly affected over time by time itself, by repetitions of seasonal changes, by cycles of drought and deluge, by traffic of people and vehicles, and by the steady growth and decay of the landscape. Control of the site is more than a geometric exercise and more than a simple, single creative act at its inception.

6.7   USE OF SITE CONSTRUCTION

Site constructions are typically created for various purposes—not the least of which is to aid in the development and control of the site form. Pavements, for example, are usually directly needed to facilitate traffic or some other activity, but—(either intentionally or unintentionally) they also affect site drainage, separation and edging of planted areas, the need for relatively flat surfaces, etc.

For highly developed sites with extensive construction, the various constructed objects may be the major determinants of the site form, possibly overwhelming or even totally displacing soil surfaces. Such is the case of urban sites that are fully built over, with plantings (if any) in freestanding or terraced containers.

At the other extreme is the virtually undisturbed site, with the bare minimum of intrusive construction. Here the effects of the construction may be virtually insignificant.

For the more typical case, the site construction plays a major, shared role in the development of the site form. Existing soil forms and manipulated, finished graded ones are also major factors. Potential functions of constructed elements with regard to their affect on site form development include the following:

Maintaining Discrete Areas. Sidewalks, drives, drainage channels, and linked buildings tend to divide the site into zones.

Achieving Three-Dimensional Forms. Construction of retaining walls, high curbs, terraces, stairs, ramps, and buildings may achieve abrupt vertical changes in the finished grade.

Achieving Changes at Site Edges. Abrupt changes at edges may be made with various forms of retaining or bracing structures.

FIGURE 6.3 The building as a functional site device

Strongly Controlling Site Drainage. Various structures frequently perform some strong channelling or other controls for drainage.

Some structures may indeed be provided *primarily* for the purpose of site
form control, retaining walls being a major example. Protection of steep em-
bankments with rip-rap or cribbing is another. These may often, however, at
the least, be developed as decorative elements of the landscape if not for any
other functional purposes.

Of all the site work performed for form development, constructed elements
tend to be the more expensive, and it is therefore desired to make the best use
of those elements that are needed for other purposes. With only minor change,
or often none, these elements can be made to serve as form-controlling elements of the landscape.

The building is, of course, often the principal constructed element that
affects site form. This relates to both horizontal and vertical site form concerns
in general, and to the potential for use of the building base as a site structure.
In a mutually supportive way, the building base may be both supported by
and provide some bracing or stabilizing functions for the site. (See Figure
6.3.)

6.8 BUILDING/SITE FORM RELATIONS

The many relations between buildings and their sites are discussed in Chapter
5. With regard to site form alone, the following are some major considerations.

Horizontal Placement of the Building

This is a major factor in the general planning of the site and, more specifically, in relating the site to its edges. The building is typically the major site "element" to be planned and more or less defines the rest of the site planning problems, except for those dealing with specific edge conditions.

The shape of the building footprint (building ground level perimeter profile) is usually strongly related to the site form, especially for tight sites where the building covers a major portion of the site surface. The building shape is both restricted by the site form and strongly limits the potential for developing other site areas.

Vertical Placement of the Building

The vertical position of the building, particularly its foundation base and ground (entry) level floor, has a major affect on the site form. The site surface development must mesh with this constraint and that of the site's defined edge conditions. Any purely sculptural manipulations of surface conditions must be done within these limits.

Vertical locations of both the edges and the buildings will also establish some conditions for other site elements—most notably sidewalks, driveways, terraces, breezeways, or other elements involving traffic of people or vehicles.

Site drainage, as it affects both the site and the building, will be strongly defined by the vertical positioning of the building. In general, it is best to direct surface drainage *away* from the building edges, especially if there are any basement spaces. However, controlled drainage on a tight site or one with problem site edge conditions may present a different situation, and building edges may actually be used as site drainage collection points that feed into a sewer system.

7

LANDSCAPING

This chapter deals briefly with the site development as a total landscape with significant concerns for other than the simple physical problems of the site. The complete development of a building site often involves a general development of its landscape. This can vary from a very light trimming of the natural site conditions to a completely redeveloped site.

There are many different possible combinations in designing responsibilities for site development work; who is specifically responsible for the landscaped design work on the site may vary from project to project depending on site conditions and the project's size and scope. The material in this chapter does not address this assignment of design responsibilities, but rather concentrates on the issues and problems related to site landscape development.

7.1 GENERAL LANDSCAPING WORK

Any landscape architects worth their salt would bridle at being categorized as dealing only with plantings and other decorative site features. The "landscape" is a total experience that relates to all the elements and relationships on a site, including those of the building/site interaction and those extending to the site periphery and its surroundings.

Landscape work typically includes general development of the site surface with plantings, walks, and various structures. There may also be piping installations for irrigation or fountains and electrical wiring for lighting. Instal-

lation of these landscaping elements must be coordinated with other construction work on the site and with the efforts of other design professionals.

One important aspect of coordinating the landscaping work is timing. Some
things must be dealt with very early in the design process, whereas some work
must be delayed until almost the end of the construction process. If existing
site features are to be preserved, preliminary investigation and landscape design work should begin early enough so that no significant site work occurs
before the features to be saved (existing trees, rock outcroppings, streams,
etc.) can be adequately protected.

Early surveys of the site—visual, photographic, and instrument generated—
should include the location and identification of the specific landscape features. Again, the intention should be to make the landscape design concerns
known *before* work proceeds on site regrading, excavations for construction,
placement of temporary construction facilities, etc. Valuable topsoil materials
should be carefully stripped from surfaces and stockpiled for later use.

In the end, of course, final touching up of the landscape is often one of the
last stages of the construction process. Good site design and construction planning should prevent the necessity to perform major regrading or installation
of deep-seated structures, piping, or wiring at this stage.

7.2 EXISTING FEATURES AND CONDITIONS

A very early assessment must be made of the potential use or preservation of
existing materials and features on the site, especially as they relate to major
site design issues or to building placement and orientation on the site. A principal reason for completing this assessment at the onset is to establish which
site elements should be retained or preserved *before* any site design or construction work occurs.

The following discussion focuses on some of the principal concerns in this
regard.

Ground Form

A principal site design issue is the form of the ground surface as it relates to
site edge conditions, proposed site uses, and the development and integration
of the building and its base with the site. These issues are discussed in Chapter
6.

Even where it may be desirable to essentially retain the existing site surface
form, it is often necessary to alter it in the construction process. Construction
activity involving traffic and the use of heavy equipment is likely to considerably disrupt the site surface conditions. If no precautions are taken, excavation for the building foundations, as well as any other large site construction, may unavoidably disrupt the site surface.

In fact, trying to retain the original site form may be the most difficult challenge and the most work in site construction. Except for conditions at the site edges, this may literally mean the *restoration*, of the site surface rather than its preservation.

To deal effectively with this issue, it is necessary first to know the initial, undisturbed condition; then to visualize the end conditions desired, and finally to understand the construction processes necessary to achieve the desired work. With all of that established it is possible to progressively plan for the preservation and/or restoration of site conditions. Of course, when the site form must be significantly or completely altered, there are many other concerns, one of which is the feasibility of using existing site materials for the reconstruction work.

Existing Site Material

As discussed in Section 4.6, the existing site materials should be viewed as an inventory of available construction materials. And as they are essentially free of cost, practical use of these materials should be carefully considered. If they are not used, the problem of what to do with them becomes a cost factor; removal and disposal can be very expensive.

For most site design concerns, the principal interest is in surface materials—that is, those in the top few feet of the ground mass. These materials relate both to existing conditions and any reconstruction work. This applies to the creation of the finished grade surface, the protection of existing plants, the installation and sustaining of new plants, and the development of bases of pavings.

However, for the development of larger site constructions and building foundations, the site materials at lower elevations are important. If these are not fully capable of providing support for the larger construction elements, it is best to determine this and provide for it very early in the design work.

Deeper ground conditions may also affect surface design concerns. There are various possible problems in this regard; and a thorough geotechnical investigation on hand will help anticipate them. A few major problems to consider are the following:

The possibility for major surface movements caused by deep ground fault conditions, unstable or unsuitable soil structures, continuous change in highly organic deposits, deep ground freezing and thawing cycles, and other natural geological phenomena.

The effects on supporting soils caused by changes in groundwater conditions. Covering most of a site with buildings and pavements may dramatically reduce water presence in the soils; continuous irrigation may dramatically increase it.

Special considerations for the use of deep foundations (driven piles, drilled piers, etc.) to support heavy construction elements. The design of (or feasibility of using) some site construction elements may be affected by the need of such support. Heavy equipment to dig deep foundations may cause considerable damage to existing surface materials.

In general, the existing site materials must be viewed as something to deal with. Use them to advantage, if possible; figure out what to do with them if they are not usable.

Special Site Features

In addition to soil materials, there may be many other site elements to consider for possible use or disposal. These may include surface vegetation, plants and trees, rock forms, drainage channels or active streams. Discussions of the problems in preserving existing elements are presented in the next section.

Special Conditions

Sites may have very special situations—being at the edge of a body of water; on steep slopes; or having portions consisting of deep ravines, swamps, unusual soils that may affect plantings, etc. These will obviously necessitate special concern in the general site planning as well as in the use of existing site materials.

7.3 PRESERVATION OF EXISTING ELEMENTS

Preservation of existing elements may be easy or difficult, depending on various factors. If elements exist on a portion of the site that is not to be developed with construction, it may be a simple matter of isolating it during construction. However, if they are to be fully incorporated into the site development, some heavily detailed plans for their protection may be required.

Extensive site construction and/or the extensive reforming of the site surface will usually greatly alter certain conditions that have fostered specific plant growths. Buildings and pavements will prevent water from penetrating the soil; this could result in problems in nourishing deeply rooted plants, most notably large trees and shrubs. Heavy compaction of soil around the base of large trees, often caused by construction work or site traffic, is a major cause of tree demise as it destroys portions of the roots. The innate structure of the plants, their long-term maintenance, and the potential effects on these plants must be considered. Severe pruning of the plants may reduce the shock of construction effects, but the means for accomplishing this cutting back and its potential feasibility must be studied by in plant growth professionals.

The tree shown in Figure 7.1 has a root system that extends considerably

FIGURE 7.1 Incorporation of existing tree in a major site development

beneath the surrounding pavements, and the small open ground around the tree may not be adequate to provide air and water to root system. Water may enter the ground beneath the tree by horizontal flow in soil layers, but a careful study of the surface and subsurface drainage and geological structure must be made to ensure this.

Figure 7.2 illustrates situations that can occur when considerable changes are made in the soil profile in the vicinity of the trees. In Figure 7.2*a* a site is raised some distance and the grade at the tree is maintained in its original position by a retaining structure that surrounds the tree. In Figure 7.2*b*, a road is below the tree and a slope-retaining structure is employed to maintain a soil mass at the level of the tree base.

For the tree in Figure 7.2*b*, the open character of the precast units used to protect the steep slope face allows air to reach the tree roots and water to seep out, preventing a hydraulic pressure buildup behind the structure. However, the excessive air plus the rapid draining of the soil may dry out the roots; to avoid this some control may be necessary, possibly involving the use of slow-draining soils or geotextiles with controlled permeability.

Natural growth characteristics of plants must be recognized and planned for the initial installation, but they must also be anticipated as maintenance concerns. One possible concern for the preservation of existing plants is compatibility with new plantings. This should be examined in the general development of the landscaping. Some plants do not like to share their space and will not endure in a heavily planted site. Others tend to demand more nutrients

(a)

(b)

FIGURE 7.2 Protection of existing trees where major vertical regrading is required

or to spread roots that choke out other growth. Still others may have different water requirements that may be incompatible with planned additional plantings.

Plants thrive in some specific relation to the sun: broadly classified as sun loving or shade loving. New installations may change this condition for existing plants. The growth of smaller plants may also be altered by shading from larger, faster-growing ones. Planned site structures or buildings may alter sun/shade affects or wind conditions on the site that can drastically change the stability of existing growth conditions.

These are very fundamental landscape design issues which can be avoided if the advice of a landscape architect or contractor is sought.

As discussed throughout this book, the entire construction process on the site must be carefully considered in terms of the measures and scheduling required to ensure proper execution of the site work. Elements to be preserved should be identified as early as possible and any measures necessary to protect them established before the site is heavily engaged in construction work. It is often helpful to seek the advice of experienced contractors regarding these matters, so that alternatives can be considered before design work is completed.

7.4 PLANNING THE LANDSCAPE

The site landscape consists of the entire formed site surface, including the soils, constructed objects, and plantings. The selection and arranging of these elements on the site is the task of landscape design and planning.

This is a major element of site design. It constitutes, almost entirely, the visual aspect of site design. However, it is not simply a matter of dealing with the *observed* site. This is not merely a display, it is an experience to be shared by the users of the site. Once a proposed design is developed, the designer must "walk through" the site, visualizing the user's experience.

This is an essential concept in landscape design—sites are not only viewed objects, but essentially participatory experiences. Participation must be considered in direct, functional ways for those who use the site for access to the buildings on it. But in a larger, more sympathetic consideration, sites may be "used" by anyone who passes by, whether they enter the site or merely observe it. This includes birds and animals as well as people, including people with a wide range of sensibilities and physical capacities.

Sites are also essentially three-dimensional, outdoor spaces, and the effects of weather, day-to-night cycles, and the seasons of the year must be visualized. The site is not going to be experienced only in the fresh cool of the morning on a balmy, sunny summer day. What will it be like in the rain? In a wind-driven snowstorm? In the dark of night? On the hottest day of the year?

Landscape planning that considers only the stage setting aspects of the single, static initial condition at installation, or deals only with pragmatic, functional requirements, or treats the site as primarily only a viewed piece of sculpture, is not fully responsible design. The site must be viewed in the context of the buildings and the general proposed site uses. The development of the site landscape offers the designer the opportunity to extend the structural/spatial aspects of the building out and into the site. Planting shrubbery and trees and placement of structures such as trellises can create enclosed or partitioned spaces that can be used to extend or accent buildings. Views can be accented, directed, blocked, framed, or otherwise controlled; traffic can be guided; settings can be established for anticipated outdoor events.

7.5 PLANTINGS

This book cannot deal with all the aspects of growing plants. The intention here is to treat some of the major aspects of plant culture and usage that influence their incorporation as site objects.

As they occur on building sites, plants are usually in one of the following basic forms. (See Figure 7.3.)

Ground Covers. These consist of low-growing plantings that are generally intended to blanket the soil surface. Grasses, creeping ivy, and junipers (low or small shrubs) are such plants. Grasses are frequently used where heavy pedestrian traffic or some play activity is anticipated. Ivy and low shrubs may be used in plant beds to help stabilize slopes and reduce erosion.

Single, Large Plants. These may be large or small trees or various forms of shrubs. Many plants can be cultivated to grow to a large size to then become singular site elements.

Controlled Plant Groupings. These may be rows of single trees, a hedge row developed with single shrubs trimmed to simulate a continuous element, or beds of various plants.

Trees exist in an almost endless variety of sizes and shapes and can be used to achieve a number of design purposes. Single trees may be freestanding elements. Groups of trees—trees of a single species and size or a mixture of species and sizes—can be arranged in rows or other formations. Growth patterns and characteristics should be recognized, especially when different species are grouped together or where planting space may be limited or confined.

Plants may be installed directly into the surface soils on site or developed in some controlled manner in a constructed container or planter. (See Figure 7.4.) Planters may be fixed in place or developed as separate, aboveground elements (flower pots, etc.). Containers must be carefully designed and the plants for them carefully selected, taking into account size, growth rate, irrigation requirements, necessary drainage, and general nutritive needs of the plants.

Actually, most cultivated plants need to be ''contained'' in some manner to maintan a controlled landscape. Landscape plantings are not static in nature; they are elements that continue to grow and change over time. What is installed today will be vastly different as time passes. Roots and plants themselves may spread out in a continuous manner and eventually take over more

(a)

(b)

FIGURE 7.3 Plant forms: (a and b) ground covers; (c) trees, large and small; (d and e) controlled groupings.

space than they are intended to occupy. This factor motivates designers to visualize the problems and needs of the initial installation and ongoing maintenance. Growth and maintenance problems are discussed in Section 7.7.

Obviously, there are many factors to consider in plant selection. Appearance is, of course, a primary concern. But the ability of plants to thrive and participate in the site conditions is critical and must be very carefully studied.

In addition to their appearance, cost, and availability, major considerations for plants are climate compatibility, cultivation needs, growth rate, toxicity, and what they may drop on the site. Site litter can be a practical concern for

(c)

(d)

(e)

FIGURE 7.3 *(Continued)*

(a)

(b)

FIGURE 7.4 Constructed plant container

trees and some shrubs, as they drop *something* all year; leaves, blossoms, dead branches, sap, etc. Their placement and relationship to various site elements require careful consideration in this regard so that potential problems can be mitigated as much as possible.

7.6 REQUIREMENTS FOR INSTALLATION OF PLANTINGS

Most plants require a soil depth and volume that will provide nourishment and growth space for the root system. The required type of soil and its total depth depends on the species and general size of the plant. Some plants can grow almost anywhere; others require very special care and handling.

Plants also need water, air, and sunlight. Again, the specific needs vary, as in the example of cactus and ferns. A specific mix of water, drainage, soil type, and sunlight will make some plants flourish and others die. Most plants require a continuous, stable amount of water; others expect to have cycles of drenching and drought; yet some require practically no water once established.

Some plants can tolerate constraint with regular trimming; others flourish with unrestricted growth. Some are generally compatible with other neighboring plants; others may need their own space or may tend to overwhelm nearby plants, invading and dominating their space and nourishment by an invasive root system and aboveground foliage.

Installation features must be carefully developed in relation to the specific form of the plantings. if specific plants are desired, the facilities must be provided to accommodate them; or, if a specific planting situation is developed in the site construction, the appropriate plantings must be carefully selected.

It is important that all factors be dealt with, including consideration for the size and nutritive needs of the plants; details of the site construction; the natural soil materials available on the site; the climate conditions at the site; water, air, and sunlight available at the site; and the orientation of plantings with respect to other site elements.

Construction for plant installations must be coordinated with other site construction. Site construction may harmfully restrict plant root growth, block sunlight, divert or drain a way needed precipitation, or cover root systems and choke off air supply. On the other hand, plant root growth may lift pavements, tilt walls, penetrate underground piping or basement, and possibly perform some jungle-like takeover of the site if no provisions are made in the design and construction, and correct maintenance is not anticipated.

A well-coordinated design involves the use of functionally required site constructions (parking dividers, curbing, retaining walls, etc.) as integral parts of the site landscape development. This can help to reduce the cost of landscape maintenance and soften the possible intrusive impact of the required construction elements on the natural site.

7.7 DESIGN FOR MAINTENANCE AND GROWTH

A major consideration in landscape design is anticipating and dealing with continual growth of plants. Plants must grow or die; growth in size must be promoted and dealt with. Since the designer deals essentially only with the initial installation, this concern must be addressed to the form of care required for the plants.

There are several directions from which to view this issue. The first and primary concern involves the specific site conditions and what is feasible to develop in terms of their limitations and construction. The site also presents some realities in terms of existing soils, water supply, climate, and existing elements to be preserved that will impact the feasibility of design proposals. And not of the least concern is the building and its uses.

A second concern is the potential level of maintenance and care that can be anticipated. For major institutional buildings, continuous, professional landscape maintenance may be assumed. In other situations it may be a case of "plant them and forget them." This seriously affects the choice of plants and the extent of feasible plantings.

In some cases it may be desirable to use specific plants, possibly in response to general community development or the owner's wishes. This sometimes results in incompatible situations: grass lawns and jungle foliage in arid desert areas; cactus in hot, humid areas; palm trees in the mountains; pines in the valleys. This is a philosophical matter for individual designers to wrestle with, but the practical aspects must be carefully handled.

In any case, designers must consider not only the immediate visual impact of their work, but also the long-term condition. What realistic level of maintenance is likely to be provided? What will the landscape look like in five or 10 years? How will possibly overgrown foliage affect neighbor's views or overhang their properties? With current concerns for potential liabilities, designers must have a concern for the long term as well as the immediate.

7.8 IRRIGATION AND SUSTENANCE

Plants must be sustained by provision of the basic elements necessary for their growth: water, air, controlled sunlight, nutrients. Protection from frost, wind, handling, and other sources of physical damage may also be concerns. Each species and individual, cultured specimen has its own needs in these regards.

While water is generally required for all plants, it must be provided in some controlled way to maintain healthy plants. Too much water can cause rot and drowning for lack of air, leaching out of soil nutrients, or erosion of supporting soils. Too little water may cause stunted growth or eventual plant death.

The manner in which plants are irrigated varies greatly by region, the character of site soils, and the type of plant materials. Many plants need only light to moderate irrigation, possibly only infrequently to supplement water from natural precipitation. Other plants demand deep, regular watering to survive.

Extensive, continued irrigation can cause major changes in the ground moisture condition of soil structures. This is especially of concern in arid regions where highly voided soils may have maintained a stability for a long time due to a low quantity of ground moisture, but can be collapsed easily if saturated.

The site soil characteristics, drainage conditions, and regional climate must be carefully examined before proceeding with the design of an irrigation system. Porous soils can absorb the irrigation water before plants can make effective use of it. Dense, slow-draining soils will possibly not absorb water; of if they do, they will hold it too long, producing rot.

Regrading may alter the surface, as well as subsurface, drainage pattern on the site, channelling water away from existing growth, that had been thriving under existing conditions. Extensive new pavements may also block or divert both water and air from the roots of existing plants. Major height change of the ground surface may either expose or excessively bury the roots of existing plants. Preservation of existing plants in general means more than simply protecting them during construction work.

New site grading and drainage patterns may produce erosion of existing of new surface soils. Runoff from both precipitation and irrigation must be carefully studied for various concerns, including erosion from planted areas.

Construction below ground must be protected from water intrusion in general if enclosed items are water sensitive. Buried electrical wiring and building basement areas are two examples. Water from extensive, continued irrigation may be critical in these cases; requiring coordination of design. This may involve reconsideration of the use of plantings that require extensive irrigation or provision of exceptionally water-resistive construction. In any case, drainage of both natural precipitation and irrigation is *always* a critical concern to be coordinated with all aspects of the site development.

8

SITE CONSTRUCTION

Development of a site may consist of reshaping the ground surface, replacing some surface materials, and introducing new plantings. However, various forms of structures may also be required. A building will constitute a major construction, but other types of structures may also be used for the site development. This chapter describes these various forms of site constructions.

8.1 SOIL STRUCTURES

Undoubtedly, the major "element" in site construction is the site itself, as constituted by the soils that define its surface and immediate subsurface layers. Creating a site as a constructed object means working extensively with the site soils. Soils have a significant impact on foundation design, pavement design, landscape design, and the general site development.

Besides providing support or encasement for various elements, soils are also used frequently for some forms of direct construction. Although topsoil, plantings, paving, or various ground covers may be used to develop surfaces, the general surface form is usually developed by the underlying soils. Achieving this general site "construction" means working with soils as construction materials. It is necessary to appreciate the need for understanding the structural character and limitations of soils.

Use of soils in various situations is discussed throughout this book. A general discussion of soils, including considerations for their general properties, classification, and structural behavior, is provided in Appendix A. The discussions in this section treat the use of soils for construction.

Development of Ground Surface Form

Development of sites often involves some considerations for the maintenance or manipulation of the ground surface form. Forms can be produced by sculpting the surface soils to a certain degree. The character of the soils immediately underlying the site surface will determine the limits on this sculpting as the sole means of achieving forms.

Most sites will house various forms of built elements that may aid in achieving the general site surface form. Some may be constructed wholly for this purpose, but others (such as the building itself) may serve major secondary functions in site form determination.

Typically, the site form is achieved with some combination of soil sculpturing and constructed elements. The remaining sections in this chapter deal with various forms of constructed site elements. The issue of achieving sloped and cut soil forms are also discussed.

Slope Control

In urban areas, as flat land becomes less available, development often spreads to more difficult sites. These sites may have steep hills or slopes or other conditions that require considerable study prior to construction. In these situations, site development and building construction often require some treatment of sloping ground surfaces. When this is necessary, a critical decision involves the maximum feasible angle of the finished slope surface (see Figure 8.1*a*).

The stability of a slope may be in question for a number of reasons. Two principal concerns relating to the soil materials are the potential for erosion of the slope face due to excessive rainfall or irrigation and the possibility of a general movement of the soil mass in a downhill direction.

A sloped surface may be generated in two different ways: cutting back of existing soil or building up with fill. The relative stability of the slope will depend largely on the character of the soils at and near the surface of the slope.

For cut slopes, the soil is largely existing and slope angle limits must be derived basically from the determination of existing soil conditions. For a relatively clean sand, the angle of repose is quite easily determined, although erosion or shock may be critical, particularly for loose sands. For rock or some very stable cemented soils, a vertical cut face or even a cave may be possible.

For most ordinary surface soils of a mixed character, the proper slope angle must be derived from studies of potential loss of the slope face by various mechanisms of failure. Slope loss by either erosion or slippage is often due

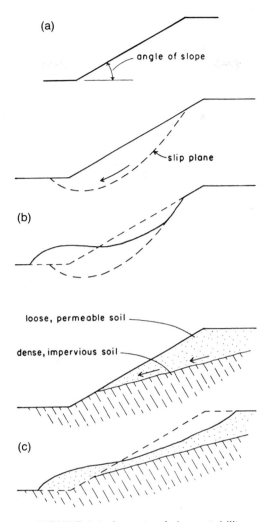

(a)

angle of slope

slip plane

(b)

loose, permeable soil

dense, impervious soil

(c)

FIGURE 8.1 Aspects of slope stability

to a combination of water soaking of the surface soils and the presence of a relatively loose soil mass. In some situations wind erosion must also be considered.

Erosion is a problem related to many considerations of the general site development. Concerns for the slope itself and the water it must drain may affect plantings, irrigation, general site contouring, pavements, and both site and building construction. Slopes may be surfaced with plantings or various pavings to protect the surface and retard erosion.

Slippage of the soil mass on the slope may occur from a number of causes. A common one is simply the vertical movement of the soil mass due to gravity, as shown in Figure 8.1*b*. This may occur as a semirotational effect along a slip plane or by the sliding of one soil mass over another, as shown in Figure

8.1*c*. These movements are typically triggered by increases in the moisture content of the soil mass.

For most ordinary situations, reasonably safe slope angle limits are established by experience and rules of thumb. Conservative limits may be established by building codes, although studies by a geotechnical expert or provision of some slope control elements may allow steeper angles.

Retaining Devices for Slopes

Slopes or abrupt changes in the ground surface elevation can be maintained or established by various means. Simple shaping of the soils may suffice if the mechanism of slope failure are acknowledged, as discussed in the preceding section. However, various other elements can be used to help, as shown in Figure 8.2.

Surface Treatments. These are basically means for keeping the surface itself in place. They do not generally affect deeper soil conditions, so they cannot be used to overcome slip plane failure or sliding, as illustrated in Figures 8.1*b* and *c*. They are generally most effective in simply retarding erosion or the massive soaking of the soil from continued precipitation. Roots of various plantings can grab a significant layer of the surface once the plantings are well established. Covering the slope surface with pavement (asphalt or concrete), individual porous pavers, coarse gravel, or large rocks may also be used. Use of geotextiles as covering can also be one factor in a total slope stabilization program.

Slopes may also be subdivided into stepped units. The ''steps'' may be quite large and individually maintained as close to flat as possible, or at least at a much shallower angle than the general slope. The ''risers'' of these steps can be any form of retaining structure appropriate to the height of the riser. Individual steps may be occupied by plantings, walkways, driveways or roads, or a series of buildings. Large developed hillsides, such as those achieved in subdivisions of homes, are often stepped up with roads and rows of buildings

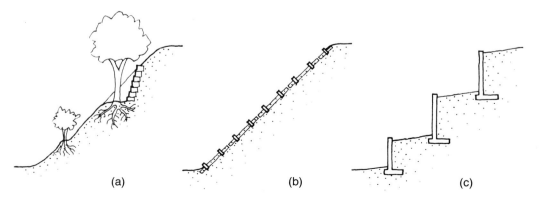

(a) (b) (c)

FIGURE 8.2 Techniques for retaining slopes

in this manner. The challenge to the site designers in these situations is to lessen the visual impact of the fabricated steps as unnatural-appearing portions of the general landscape.

Temporary Bracing

Various expedient methods may be used to maintain soil profiles during construction or general site development. Deep excavations for buildings or general construction on steep slopes may utilize these methods.

Shallow excavations can often be made with no provision for bracing the sides of the excavation. However, when the cut is quite deep, the soil has little cohesive character (loose sand, for example), or the undercutting of adjacent construction or property is a concern, some form of bracing for the cut faces may be required.

One means of bracing consists of driving steel sheetpiling to form a wall to allow soil to be removed from one side, as shown in Fig. 8.3a. As with

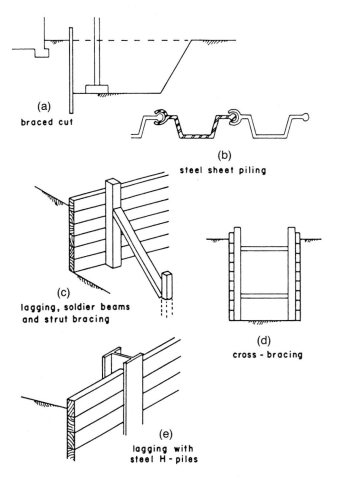

(a)
braced cut

(b)
steel sheet piling

(c)
lagging, soldier beams
and strut bracing

(d)
cross - bracing

(e)
lagging with
steel H - piles

FIGURE 8.3 Temporary bracing

other temporary walls of this nature, the piling may stay in place, possibly to be used as the forming for one side of a cast concrete wall. However, if possible, these expensive piling units can be withdrawn for reuse.

Another form of bracing wall is one constructed with vertical beams or posts (called soldiers) and horizontal boards or sheets (called lagging), as shown in Figures 8.3c, d, and e. This construction may be achieved by driving the soldiers as piles, but is more often done by building the wall downward as the excavation proceeds.

Both sheetpile walls and those using soldiers and lagging generally need some form of bracing themselves. This may take the form of crosshole braces, as shown in Figure 8.3d, or individual struts (called rakers), as shown in Figure 8.3c. For walls intended for permanent installation, where soil conditions permit, bracing may be done through the wall and into the soil mass with drilled-in anchors.

Major bracing of excavations is frequently required with construction in tight urban site situations, especially when the site is surrounded by existing streets or buildings. Its development must be done as a coordinated effort with the general foundation and site construction work.

8.2. PAVEMENTS

Paved surfaces may be achieved with various materials, common ones described as follows:

Concrete. This is usually the strongest form of paving and can be used for heavy traffic-bearing roads or simple walks. Concrete paving slabs are typically placed over a thin layer of gravel, crushed rock, or sand to provide a good base and a draining layer beneath the pavement. Minimal reinforcement may be provided with a single layer of steel wire fabric; thicker pavements may be reinforced with two-way grids of steel rods.

Asphalt. Various forms of concrete produced with an oil-based binder (tar, etc.) can be used. Materials, thickness, and base preparation depend on the desired degree of permanence and cost limitations.

Loose Unit Pavers. Bricks, cobblestones, cast interlocking asphalt or concrete units, cut wood sections, or other elements may be laid over a sand and gravel base. This is a traditional and ancient form of paving and can be very durable if installed properly and made with good quality elements.

Loose Materials. Fine gravel, pulverized bark, or wood chips may be used for walks or areas with light traffic. These generally require some ongoing maintenance to preserve the surface, but can be very practical and blend well with natural features of a site (existing surfaces, plantings, etc.). Loose surfacing can also reduce moisture loss by evaporation from surface soils and may help reduce loss of surfaces from erosion due to wind or heavy rains.

Areas to be paved must be graded (recontoured) to some level below the desired finished surface to allow for the installation of the paving. If existing site materials are undesirable for the pavement base, it may be necessary to cut down to a lower surface elevation and import materials to build up a better base for the pavement.

Pavements, especially the solid forms of concrete or asphalt, result in considerable surface runoff during rainfall, which must be carefully considered in the general investigation of site surface drainage. The issue of runoff disposal or control of irrigation for plantings can be critical in general site design development.

Concrete Slabs

The usual means of achieving a working surface for sidewalks, driveways, basement floors, and floors for buildings without basements is to cast concrete directly over some prepared base on top of the soil. As shown in Figure 8.4, the typical construction for this consists of the following components:

1. A prepared soil surface, graded to the desired level and compacted to avoid subsidence.
2. A coarse-grained pavement base, usually predominantly fine gravel and coarse sand, also compacted to some degree if more than a few inches thick. Three or 4 in. is common for floor slabs; a minimum of 2 in. is common for exterior pavements.
3. A membrane of reinforced, water-resistant paper or thick plastic film (6 mil minimum) used where moisture intrusion is a critical concern.
4. The concrete slab.

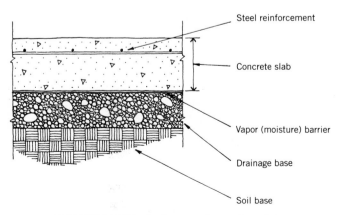

FIGURE 8.4 Typical concrete paving slab

5. Steel reinforcement, often of heavy gage wire mesh with steel rods at edges.

While the basic construction process is quite simple, there are various considerations that must be addressed in developing details and specifications for the construction.

Thickness of Pavements.   For residences and other situations with light traffic, a common thickness is a nominal 4-in. slab; actually 3.5 in., if standard lumber 2 × 4s are used as edge forms. With proper reinforcement and good concrete, this is an adequate slab for most purposes.

Where some vehicular traffic is anticipated, or where other heavy concentrated loads, such as those from tall, heavy partitions, are expected, it may be desirable to jump to the next logical thickness of 5.5 in., based on the use of 2 × 6s as edge forms. At this thickness, it may be possible to avoid providing individual wall footings for nonstructural partitions, a simplification in construction employed probably to justify the cost of additional concrete and reinforcement for the slabs.

For very heavy trucks, storage warehouses, or other situations involving heavy concentrated loads, thicker pavements and greater reinforcement may be necessary. However, the nominal 4-in. and 6-in. slabs account for most building floors.

Reinforcement.   For 4-in. slabs reinforcement is usually accomplished with welded wire mesh. For thicker slabs, or as an alternative for 4-in. slabs, small diameter rebars (No. 3 or No. 4) may be used with somewhat wider spacings than those in the wire mesh. Even when mesh is used, some extra rebars may be provided at edges or steps, around openings, or at other critical locations.

The purpose of the reinforcement is to reduce cracking of the concrete, due primarily to shrinkage during curing, differential volume changes due to temperature changes, and some unequal settlement of the pavement base. Cracking is especially undesirable in the top (exposed surface) or the slabs, so the reinforcement should be supported during casting to be relatively close to the top surface.

Another means of reinforcing, or basically altering, the concrete is the addition of fiber materials to the mix, which is a growing practice for all exposed slabs. In cases where considerable movement of the base is expected, pavements may need to be prestressed or developed as framed systems on grade.

Joints.   It is generally desirable to pour paving slabs in small units to control shrinkage cracking. For floor slabs of buildings, this results in construction joints, which may not relate well to floor finish materials. Where permanent wall construction is established, joints should be located at these points rather than in the middle of floor spaces.

For exterior paving, joints should occur quite frequently; they should be appropriate to the pavement width and thickness, and generally replaceable if units settle or crack easily. Joints should also be placed at what are predictable locations for cracks, such as changes in width, intersections, corners, etc. Extreme outdoor temperature range or anticipated soil settlements may also affect the frequency of joints.

Larger pours can be made if control joints are formed or cut in the slab. Movements at these joints may be small for interior floors, but they should still be located at points that will not cause problems with floor finishes.

Surface Treatment.   If the top of a paving slab is to be exposed to wear, it should be specially formed for this purpose during casting of concrete. A hard, smooth surface is generally desired, one typically developed by fine trowelling with a steel trowel and possibly the addition of some hardening materials to the finished surface.

For a slip-resistance surface (now a general safety requirement in all public traffic areas) intended to reduce accidents when a pavement is wet, a grit material may be added to the surface or a deliberately roughened surface developed (broomed, sandblasted, etc.). Smoothness is also generally not highly desirable when other finish materials are to be used, especially ones that must be attached with adhesives. In the latter case, the steel trowelling may be omitted, as a rough levelling of the surface is acceptable.

Other Paving Materials

Concrete pavements are highly durable and effective for heavy traffic. They are, however, quite expensive if correctly installed, so other forms may be used for economic reasons or to achieve a different form of surface. Of course, most of these can be developed on top of a concrete slab, as they might be when used on the roof of an underground structure. The following discussion, however, deals primarily with the use of other paving materials in place of a concrete slab.

Figure 8.5 shows a variety of pavings used in place of the common concrete slab. These basic forms are discussed as follows.

Asphalt.   Asphalt paving is essentially a form of concrete (sand, gravel, and a binder) made with a bituminous binder instead of portland cement. However, it is typically a built-up layer with a somewhat denser, smoother topping developed for the top surface. It is naturally less permeable (allowing water penetration) than ordinary concrete, although rapid water accumulation during heavy rains will flow off a sloping surface of either concrete or asphalt at about the same rate.

As with a concrete slab, a base should be developed for a good asphalt pavement. However, for lightly trod walks, a very thin coating of the ground with only a minimally developed base may suffice. Asphalt surfaces are some-

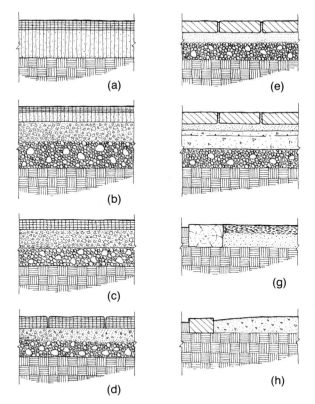

FIGURE 8.5 Miscellaneous paving materials

what less durable than hardened concrete, and constant traffic and exposure to weather will wear them down. Surfaces can be repaired or restored with additional coatings on top of the old paving. However, topping does not ensure the structural integrity of the basic paving or its base.

Unit Pavers.   Ancient pavings were developed with stones laid to produce a relatively smooth surface. Very fine surfaces were developed with cut stones, and the floors over soil in many great works of architecture were developed as loose stone paving over a crushed gravel base.

Later, bricks and fired clay tiles were used in the same manner as cut stones. Matched sets of smooth field stones were used to produce cobblestone paving.

As with any paving of loose units, the application may be made essentially directly over soil or developed more permanently. Bricks or tile, for example, may be set in mortar over a concrete slab for a really permanent, stable pavement.

In addition to stone, bricks, and tile, just about any hard elements can be used for paving. Wood blocks, planks, timbers, or cut sections of logs can be used. So can precast concrete units, now most commonly used when installation is directly in the ground.

Complete details for unit paving will vary depending on the units themselves, regional concerns, the traffic to be borne, and what is underneath the paving. Selection of the units is usually a landscape design decision, but it is also influenced by the availability of materials, local weather, and the general economics of the project.

Loose Materials. For some forms of traffic, or for special surfaces such as racetracks, playgrounds, or playing fields, different types of loose materials can be used for a developed surface. Widely spaced unit pavers may be used with an infill of grass for a form of paved lawn. Other nongrassy areas can be developed with pulverized bark, wood chips, fine gravel, or various mixtures of soil materials.

Natural soil surfaces may form relatively hard, durable crusts in some cases, or be encouraged to do so with some help. Adding some fine silt or dry clay to an existing sand or gravel surface, combined with watering or compaction, may produce such a surface.

Grass alone, when carefully cultivated and maintained, can form a type of pavement. Besides sustaining some degree of traffic, it may serve to effectively prevent surface erosion, improve precipitation runoff, or otherwise do what is generally expected from other forms of paving.

Framed Pavements

In some situations, it is necessary to develop a paved surface for which the stability of the supporting ground cannot be firmly established. One common situation of this kind occurs when a building floor slab must be placed on considerable fill. Foundations for the building columns and walls will hopefully be supported with more stability, so the problem becomes one of relative settlement of the floor with respect to other construction.

Of course, methods exist for consolidation of fill materials, but they are quite labor intensive and must be achieved in relatively thin, successive layers. The greater the total vertical thickness of the fill, the less feasible compaction becomes.

One method of dealing with this problem is simply to develop the pavement (usually a concrete slab) as a spanning, reinforced concrete structure. Possible forms for this area are shown in Figure 8.6. For relatively short spans, beams may be formed as simple trenches and cast as one with the slab (Figure 8.6a). For larger spans, or when considerable fill is placed (often the major reason for developing the structure), it may be more feasible to form and cast beams first, as shown in Figure 8.6b.

Light partition walls may usually be supported on concrete floor slabs on grade without special provision. Walls used as bearing walls, or simply any walls of heavy construction, should have some more developed support, essentially a wall footing. The construction shown in Figure 8.6 may also be used for this purpose in some situations.

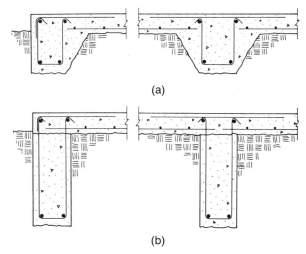

(a)

(b)

FIGURE 8.6 Framed pavements

8.3   RETAINING STRUCTURES

Site development frequently involves the use of various retaining structures. These help to achieve abrupt changes in the ground surface elevation. The form of structure often relates primarily to the height of the elevation change on the two sides of the retaining structure.

The smallest retaining structures are curbs, which may take various forms, as shown in Figure 8.7. Curbs are edging devices that define the boundary

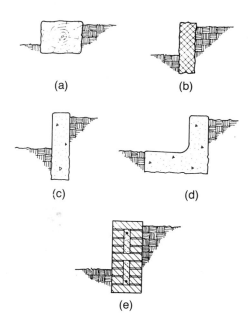

(a)   (b)

(c)   (d)

FIGURE 8.7 Forms of curbs   (e)

between different units of the site surface. They are frequently placed at the edges of pavements and thus relate to the paving materials and forms. The form of drainage of the pavement may also affect the details of the curb.

Curbs are usually limited to elevation changes of less than 18 in. or so. As the height of the retaining structure increases, a different general form of construction is required.

Loose-Laid Retaining Walls

For abrupt elevation changes of more than 18 in., some form of wall construction is required. This may be achieved with loose-laid stones (without mortar) or other elements, as shown in Figure 8.8. Such construction must be banked, or leaned, into the cut to resist the horizontal force of the soil on the high side of the wall.

Walls of this type can be very effective and simple to construct. Executed with field stone or timber they may be quite attractive, especially when used with other largely natural materials such as earthen surfaces or plantings.

A typical advantage of the loose-laid wall is its natural porosity, which allows groundwater to seep through. This is especially critical when plantings on the high side are regularly and heavily irrigated.

Cantilever Retaining Walls

The strongest retaining structures for achieving abrupt elevation changes are *cantilever retaining walls*, which consist of structural walls of masonry or

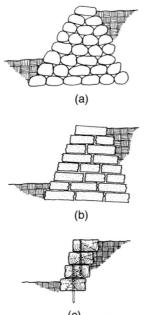

(a)

(b)

(c)   **FIGURE 8.8** Loose-laid retaining walls

concrete anchored to a large footing. Some common forms are those shown in Figure 8.9.

Figure 8.9*a* shows a form used for walls up to approximate 6 ft high. (Height refers to the ground surface elevation difference on the two sides of the wall.) Critical structural concerns are the rotational, overturning effect and the horizontal sliding effect, both of which are caused by the horizontal soil pressure on the high side of the wall. The dropped portion of the footing

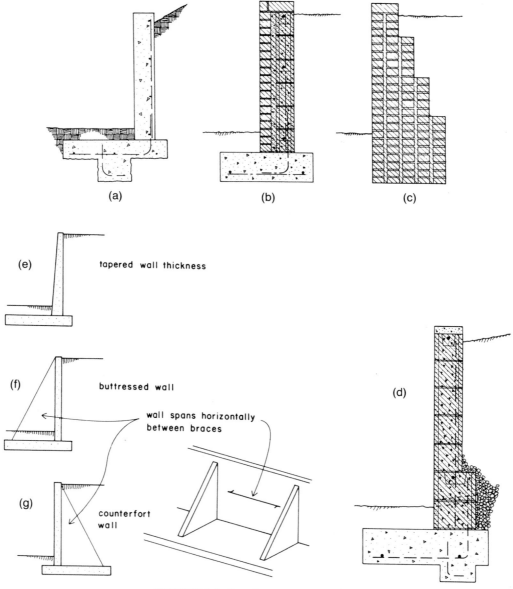

(a)   (b)   (c)

(e)   tapered wall thickness

(f)   buttressed wall

        wall spans horizontally
        between braces

(d)

(g)   counterfort
        wall

FIGURE 8.9 Cantilever retaining walls

(called a shear key) is commonly used to enhance the resistance to horizontal sliding.

Short walls may be achieved with masonry or concrete. If built with concrete, both the wall and the footing are usually reinforced as shown in Figure 8.9a. Masonry walls may be constructed similarly, as shown in Figure 8.9b, or may be developed as gravity walls, which rely strictly on their dead weight to resist the overturning effects, as shown in Figure 8.9c.

Gravity retaining walls are still frequently used where large units of stone are available. The all brick construction shown in Figure 8.9c is an ancient form, probably not applicable in most situations today unless a mass of unmatched recycled bricks are available. The gravity wall of stone may generally resemble the form of the loose-laid wall in Figure 8.8a, except for the addition of mortar between the units. Another form of the gravity wall is that using large stones cast into a concrete wall.

As walls get taller, it is common to use a tapered wall form. Concrete walls are evenly tapered, as shown in Figure 8.9d, while masonry walls are typically step-tapered, using regular units of the masonry, as shown in Figure 8.9e.

Tall retaining walls may also be braced by buttresses or fin walls perpendicular to the retaining wall, as shown in Figure 8.9f and g. If built on the back side, these do not effect the the visible side of the wall; however, building them on the exposed, low side is usually easier and more economical as it involves less excavation and backfill on the high side.

Retaining walls may also be developed as parts of building construction; they are building walls with a portion of the wall bracing provided by other elements of the building construction. The typical basement wall is generally a retaining structure, although not usually of the cantilever type, as it works by spanning the basement and first floor, which brace it laterally.

Miscellaneous Retaining Structures

There are many additional forms of retaining structures; some employ ancient forms and others utilize new technologies. Ancient structures include those developed with stone construction of both rough and finally detailed forms. Many basic systems developed with stone have been translated into concrete in more recent times, utilizing units of precast concrete. The following examples include several priority systems used to develop porous-faced retaining structures (see Figure 7.2b).

Timber is still used in both classic forms and new situations, made possible by the utilization of newer technologies that employ tiebacks and anchors with geotechnical fabrics, drilled-in anchors, etc.

The choice of rough stone and timber structures is frequently based on aesthetic considerations as well as practical utilization because they blend well with other natural landscape materials. Simulation of older forms and materials, executed in concrete or various composite materials, is often a feature of newer products and systems.

Where simple practicality dominates and aesthetic issues are of less concern, there are many pragmatic alternatives for both temporary and permanent construction of structures. Use of temporary bracing systems is described in Section 8.1. Although used for expedient progress of the construction, temporary structures sometimes remain in place as built or are incorporated into more permanent forms of construction. Thus a sheet pile wall used to achieve excavation may become the form for one side of a basement or cantilever retaining wall.

A sometime used retaining structure is the *gabion*, which consists of formed wire baskets filled with large stones. Individual baskets are treated as individual blocks or units and are strung in rows and stacked up to form structures.

8.4 PLANTERS

Plants occur in great variety—from general ground cover such as grass to large trees. Establishing plants and promoting their continued life and growth are multifaceted concerns. A particularly critical one related to site design is that of establishing the limits for the root production or basic spread of growth. This may be visualized in construction terms as the design of some restricting construction element or device.

Restriction of ground cover plants usually requires some form of edging. This may simply consist of a defined trim line that is regularly controlled by trimming (see Figure 8.10). However, more common is some actual construc-

FIGURE 8.10 Planting edge developed simply as a maintenance task

tion, against which the horizontal spread of growth can be arrested, although trimming may also be required.

A simple form of edging is shown in Figure 8.11. Edging may be simple and functional or highly decorative and elaborate. The edging devices may serve the singular purpose of controlling and maintaining the plantings, but frequently satisfy other purposes. The tops of curbs and retaining walls, edges of sidewalks and drives, and faces of building foundation walls often define the edges of planting areas.

Occasionally it is necessary to define planting in a more complete fashion. This may extend literally to the creation of an individual planter device, such as a large container (a pot or bowl). One reason for this is to establish some planting on top of a structure or a paved area. Figure 8.12 shows the development of plantings on top of a concrete structure in conjunction with a general plaza area. A concrete wall form is used for the planter and also accommodates seating attached to its face. In the upper figure, a relatively shallow planter is developed for small plants, while the lower figure shows a deep planter, adequate for small trees.

Where planters are permanently installed, such as those shown in Figure 8.12, provisions must be made for some form of continuous irrigation and a piped drainage system. Plantings in this case will eventually outgrow the planter and must be replaced, although careful trimming and selection of slow-growing plants will lessen this problem.

Planters such as those illustrated in Figure 8.12 can also be installed in the ground. These may consist only of the edge walls, although in some situations it may also be desirable to contain root growth for various reasons.

(a)

FIGURE 8.11 Edging for planted areas

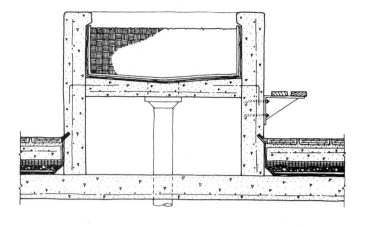

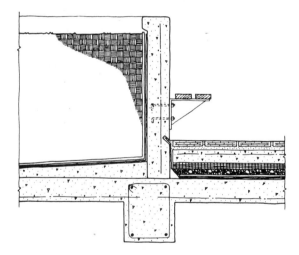

FIGURE 8.12 Planters developed on top of spanning structures

Planters may also literally consist of big pots that simply sit somewhere and are potentially moveable. They may or may not be actually moved, but their construction is nevertheless relatively independent of what they sit on. In this situation watering is most likely done by hand tending and drainage by simply controlled leaking. Overwatering and regular drainage must be anticipated and allowances made in establishing the locate of these planters.

Figure 8.13 shows a variety of individual, freestanding planters, varying from simple flower pots to large, most likely unmoveable containers. The use of different types of freestanding planters offers the designer the opportunity to integrate the building with the landscape: the landscape enters the building and the building is extended to join the general site landscape. The result is a more gradual transition from the constructed site to the natural site.

(a)

(b)

(c)

FIGURE 8.13 Freestanding planters

8.5 SITE SERVICE ELEMENTS

Various elements are required to perform utilitarian tasks on a site. Signs, fire hydrants, water drainage control devices and meters, and large electrical transformers required for building services must be incorporated into the general site development. The following are some functional elements that often require planning.

Channels

Ground surface drainage tends to become focused into channels. Following natural ground contours, natural channels eventually collect to form creeks and rivers. For developed sites it is usually necessary to form new channels as part of the surface drainage design.

Constructed channels may be closed, in the form of piping or tunnels for sewers. In some cases, however, open channels may be formed to feed into existing sewer systems or into natural rivers or lakes. Open channels may be shaped basically as ground forms, but usually have a lining on the bottom and/or sides to prevent washouts and gradual erosion.

Figure 8.14 shows the forms for various types of open channels. For landscaped sites, the channels may be developed as natural-appearing streams, and some appropriate, attractive construction may be used for the channels; in keeping with other site construction materials.

The strongest channels are usually those made of reinforced concrete construction, such as that shown in Figure 8.14c. These may be used as more positive control against erosion, or perhaps are required where major flow is anticipated due to local rainstorm conditions.

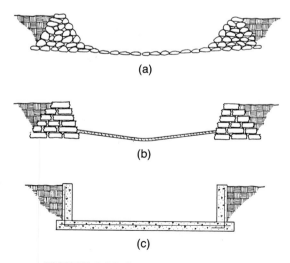

(a)

(b)

(c)

FIGURE 8.14 Constructed channels

Constructed channels are most often parts of some general regional flood control or storm drainage system. They may already exist on a site, even if other development has not been achieved. In any event, they usually have connections off the individual site, and their design, alteration, or simply their utilization is subject to various controls.

Tunnels

Site development for large projects usually involves some use of underground tunnels.

Sewers. Small sewers usually consist of buried piping: steel, cast iron, fiber-reinforced plastic, or fired clay. As the required flow capacity increases, larger pipes may be used, but some form of tunnel construction can also be used.

Utilities. For various reasons, services such as gas, water, electrical power, and telephone lines may be delivered through tunnels. One reason for this is the ease with which continuous maintenance and alterations can be achieved.

Pedestrian or Vehicular Traffic. Connections between associated separate buildings in climates with extremely cold weather are now often made with underground tunnels. Tunnel networks may also be used for rail lines, waste collection, delivery systems, and various other purposes.

Tunnel construction may be simple for small tunnels that are a short distance below grade. However, any tunnel construction must be coordinated with other site development work and the development of building foundation systems. Where site planting is developed, the tops of tunnels must be sufficiently buried to allow for the plant growth over them.

Utility Elements and Enclosures

Many site services, while predominantly underground (water, gas, etc.), have control devices or equipment that are above ground for ease of access or maintenance. Examples are electrical transformers and meters, shutoff valves and meters for gas and water, and water supply and controls for firefighting. Placement of these elements is restricted, often due partly to the locations of off-site mains and building entry points.

Some building service elements and equipment may also be outside the building. This may include air intake or exhaust elements, cooling towers or other items for air conditioning systems, or entry manholes or access doors to underground vaults or tunnels. Regular trash pickup generally involves outdoor locations for trash collection and storage.

Equipment may be freestanding or enclosed. Enclosures may be visually enhanced and incorporated into the general landscape, but some specific detail requirements must be recognized.

8.6 STAIRS AND RAMPS

Some sites are virtually flat, requiring essentially only smooth paved surfaces for pedestrian traffic. However, many sites require the facilitation of some relatively abrupt vertical movement, involving the use of ramps or stairs.

Hardly any paved site surfaces are truly dead flat because of the simple need for drainage. Paving for essentially flat surfaces must be minimally pitched (flat, but sloped) or crowned (arched) to provide for reasonably quick drainage. However, what is required for minimum drainage will hardly be noticeable to pedestrians as a sloped surface.

Ramps

The precise distinction between a sloped sidewalk and a ramp is somewhat blurred. Ramps are generally classified as such for angles between about 5 and 15 degrees. Limits on the steepness of the slope depend on specific code requirements, especially those for use by handicapped persons. Figure 8.15 provides some data with regard to the layout of ramps and stairs.

A critical concern for all paved surfaces is their condition of slipperiness when wet. This becomes increasingly critical when the surfaces are sloped. Thus real ramped surfaces should have some considerable traction, which can be achieved in the choice of surfacing materials. Specifications for this may be controlled by codes in some situations. Concrete surfaces may be deliberately roughened or have some grit materials added to their surfaces. Tiles and other unit pavers usually are rated for some degree of controlled surface traction when wet.

For ramps that rise some significant distance, handrails may be required. This may also be a code requirement, but should be studied in terms of the users, placement of the ramps, and the presence or absence of edge construction such as walls.

Stairs

For safety reasons, exterior stairs are usually made slightly shallower in slope than interior stairs. However, a minimum step height is also desired, since a very low riser is likely to trip pedestrians. Actually, a single step, regardless of height, is dangerous unless some clear signal is given as to its presence.

Outdoor stairs can be achieved by a variety of constructions, depending on traffic, structural support, and general site development. Concrete stairs may

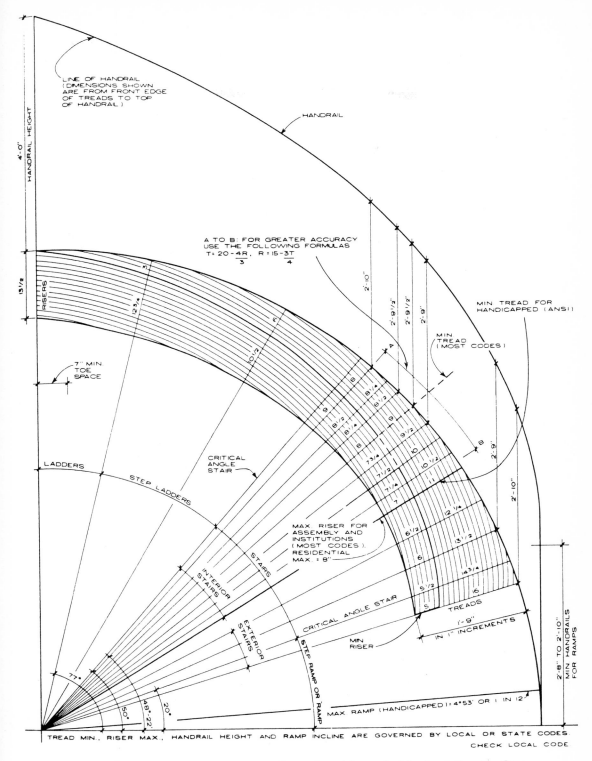

FIGURE 8.15 Data for stair layout. Reproduced from *Architectural Graphic Standards*, 8th ed., with permission of the publishers, John Wiley & Sons.

FIGURE 8.16 Site steps developed with timber and loose paving

be developed as pavements, resting on a soil base, or as framed structures on grade.

Stairs with surfacing of stone, brick, precast concrete, or ceramic tile can be developed with unit pavers on top of a concrete substructure. However, unit pavers may also be used to develop a stepped, paved surface directly on supporting soil. The latter is more likely for very shallow stairs.

Figure 8.16 shows the development of what may be considered a very shallow sloped stair or stepped ramp. Pieces of treated wood timbers (possibly railroad ties) are used to define risers, with the general tread surface developed with loose paving material compacted to a wearing surface.

Stairs or ramps may also be developed with a continuity of paving elements that also form walks or terraced surfaces, as shown in Figure 8.17.

For general safety, stairs should have some form of handrail and preferably be lighted for night use.

8.7   CONSTRUCTION AS SITE SCULPTURE

Many of the constructed elements on a site are required for functional reasons. Their basic form and placement on the site may be controlled by engineering design requirements. Development of the site in general must incorporate all of these functional devices. If the site is designed as a viewed object with concern for aesthetic values, the presence of these objects must be treated.

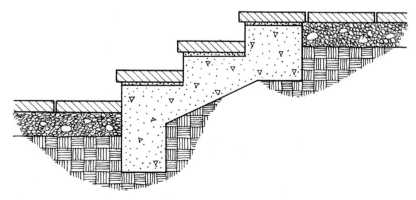

FIGURE 8.17 Site stairs developed with continuous path pavement construction

There are various approaches to dealing with the "necessaries" on a site with regard to improving appearance. (See Figure 8.18.)

1. They may be aesthetically improved through the use of some finish enhancement or manipulation of their form while retaining functionality.
2. They may be incorporated into the landscape and made to serve landscape design purposes, as plant edging, planters, paved surfaces, seating, etc.
3. They may be hidden from view by covering them or screening them with planting, fences, or other site construction.

(a)

(b)

FIGURE 8.18 Site elements incorporated into site design

There is nothing wrong with any of these solutions. Indeed, all—plus other tricks—can be used on a single site. In the end, what is desired is the accomplishment of the following:

The viewed site is as handsome as possible.

Functional needs are met with reasonable performance and safety.

The whole site development is achieved with the minimum investment of money and effort.

8.8 UNDERGROUND BUILDINGS

Site surfaces are sometimes developed over entirely underground building spaces. This may occasionally occur with an entire underground building, but more commonly involves a portion of the extended basement of a building. A frequent occurrence of this type involves the development of underground parking for a building, in which the parking structure may exist below a major portion of the site, while the building above the ground is over only a portion of the site.

Development of the site in this case generally involves three basic concerns:

Excavation and construction for the underground constructed building. If this is entirely below the original site grade, this may involve considerable removal of existing soil materials.

Redevelopment of the general finished surface grade. This will ordinarily involve considerable backfill around the construction as well as some buildup on top of the structure.

Development of the finished surface of the site: plantings, paved surfaces, etc.

A major concern for underground spaces is an overhead structure that is *not* simply the floor of a building above. This structure, which we call the roof of the underground space, may support soil of some thickness or be directly paved over as a terrace or plaza surface. With an extensive underground construction and major landscape development, all possible overhead conditions may exist.

Structure

Compared to ordinary roofs, those for underground spaces usually carry many times the total gravity loads. The construction of the structure itself is likely to be among the heaviest types of sitecast concrete. Add to that either a heavy load of soil or the high live load usually required for a terraced roof area or a plaza (150 to 250 psf in most codes).

A further concern is often that of restricting the total depth of the structure in order to keep the depth of the underground construction to a minimum. All of this conspires to generally keep spans short, with the possible goal of effecting some efficiency in the spanning systems. The usual options for sitecast concrete floor systems are all possible, although a few tend to be more feasible. Among these, the two-way flat slab and two-way waffle systems usually offer the smoothest underside and least overall depth; they are favored, especially if the underside of the structure is left exposed.

Water Control

A roof is a roof, and the basically flat roof of an underground structure is not significantly different from any flat roof. A totally watertight membrane is required, together with all flashing and careful sealing of any penetrations. The membrane must be protected (especially here) and some insulation and a vapor barrier may be indicated.

Drainage is somewhat different here than for a conventional roof, but not any less indicated. The form of drainage will relate somewhat to what is above the roof—soil or paving—and probably to the development of a total drainage system for the whole underground construction. As in other situations, the roof must be drained essentially by gravity flow, involving considerations for the total slopes required and the vertical dimensions of the construction necessary to achieve drainage and water removal.

As for walls and floors, concern for the watertight security of the underground space may be heightened if the space is occupied by people or moisture-sensitive equipment. However, there is hardly any middle ground for a watertight roof—it is truly watertight or it isn't, so this is less a variable issue than it is for basement walls and floors in ordinary circumstances.

Earth-Covered Roofs

An especially critical water control problem is that of the roof supporting earth and plantings. The earth may get wet from precipitation alone, but the plantings will require continuous moisture, so the water condition will be ever present. But drainage must be effective to prevent a saturated, rot-inducing condition for the plant roots.

Another major consideration in this situation is the provision of sufficient depth of earth fill for sustaining the planting. This may be minimal for grass, but of major proportions for trees. To save depth, large plants and trees may be placed in special deepened or raised planters integrated into the space of an otherwise not so deep underground construction.

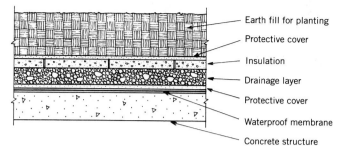

FIGURE 8.19 Development of an earth-covered roof

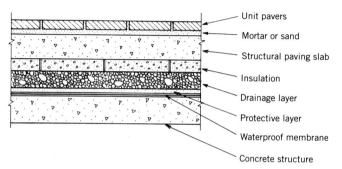

FIGURE 8.20 Plaza pavement over a spanning structure

Figure 8.19 shows some of the features of an earth-covered underground structure, sustaining only minimal plantings in this case.

Paved Roofs

When close to the surface, underground spaces may have paved roofs that form terraces or plazas for buildings or simply parts of a general site development. Extensive underground parking garages are developed in many locations with parks, squares, or other open spaces on their roofs. Paving here is not essentially different from other outdoor paving with all the usual options. The sub-base and general support may be somewhat different and must be generally integrated with the overall construction of the roof of the space below. Figure 8.20 shows the typical components of a plaza pavement over an underground structure.

The same underground space may have both earth for plantings and paving on different areas of the roof. If the constructed roof is essentially flat, some coordination of the overall dimensions for development of the two types of surfaces is warranted.

9

SPECIAL CONCERNS
FOR SITES

This chapter presents a number of special problems and issues regarding the development of building sites.

9.1 LIGHTING

Electrically powered outdoor lighting may serve various purposes. Sometimes several different purposes can be fulfilled with the use of a single fixture. It is important to understand the different kinds of illumination needs in order to accurately judge the value and appropriateness of the many different lighting systems.

General Illumination

It is sometimes desirable to provide general, overall lighting of an area of the site, possibly of the entire site (see Figure 9.1). The size of the area and the level of illumination intensity required will depend on the reason for the lighting.

The most common form of general lighting is a fixture, or series of spaced fixtures, with the lighting source on top of a pole or tower structure. The nature of the illumination provided in this manner depends on several considerations, outlined as follows. (See Figure 9.2.)

FIGURE 9.1 Lighting system for general site illumination

Height of the Fixtures. Light intensity decreases rapidly as the distance from the source increases; thus, the higher the fixture, the less illumination it will deliver at ground level. However, the higher the source, the wider the area it will affect.

Spacing of Fixtures. Widely spaced fixtures will result in local bright spots with a falloff of illumination between them; closely spaced fixtures can produce a relatively uniform illumination.

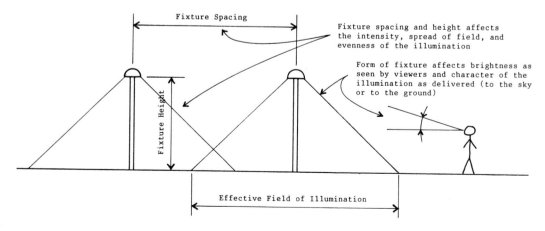

FIGURE 9.2 Aspects of a general illumination system

Form of the Fixtures. Individual types of fixtures emit a characteristic form of light. A principal concern is the direction in which light is delivered; for general illumination, this is usually downward from a high fixture. However, elements of the fixture can also affect the light in various other ways: for example, aiming it narrowly as a spotlight effect.

Type of Lighting Element (Lamp). The lighting element used (incandescent bulb, fluorescent tube, mercury vapor, etc.) will affect the character of the illumination provided in various ways, such as:

the amount (intensity) of light, depending on the type of lamp and its wattage

the color of the light (reddish for incandescent, bluish for ordinary fluorescent, etc.)

the spectral character (soft, harsh, etc.)

These are the principal considerations to be made in selecting of a general illumination system, although other factors may be influential in some cases. Other major concerns are maintenance and long-term operating costs.

Illumination of the Building Exterior

Sometimes it is desired to illuminate the exterior of the building to make it more visible at night. This can be achieved in a number of ways, including the placement of light fixtures directly on the building exterior. However, fixtures may also be placed on the site—as spot lights aimed at the building, or to serve dual functions for other site lighting tasks, such as general illumination.

The form of lighting system used for this purpose obviously depends on the size and shape of the building and the specific reasons for illuminating it. It will also depend on the other types of lighting provided on the site and how these light sources interact. For example, a lot of light thrown on the exterior of a light-colored building will probably provide considerable general illumination for the immediate area around the building, like it or not.

Illumination of Traffic Paths

Driveways and walks are often illuminated for night use. This may be achieved with general area illumination or, more specifically, by a system for this sole purpose. A critical concern here is to fulfill the direct purpose of lighting the paths to ensure greater safety and ease. Therefore, it is necessary to concentrate on illuminating the *path* and to avoid distracting or blinding the user. This may affect the placement and/or the form of the fixtures, as shown in Figure 9.3.

Where signage is used to direct the pathways, its viewing should be developed carefully for both daylight and night viewing conditions.

(a)

(b)

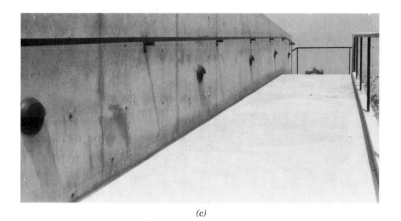

(c)

FIGURE 9.3 Pathway lighting elements

Security Lighting

Site lighting is often provided in part for security concerns. People feel they are—and probably truly are in most cases—safer in brightly lit environments when outdoors at night. Conversely, burglars or other persons of questionable intentions may be reluctant to approach a building whose exterior and site are brightly lit.

This is an issue that generally affects the sense of security of a single property owner or a whole neighborhood or community. It may also be specifically required for some situations, such as high crime areas, military installations, etc.

Specific Object and Accent Illumination

Site lighting is often provided for the specific purpose of night viewing an object on the site. The object may be a building, a sculpture, or other attractive item.

If the property is not generally used at night, this may be the only site lighting. The illuminated object may be a sign or other element that identifies the property or serves an advertising purpose.

However, the lighting for a featured object may also be in a generally illuminated part of the site and created as an exercise in relative intensity, with a soft, low level of general illumination and a bright spot on the object. This may also be done for functional purposes, for example to highlight the building entrance.

Decorative Lighting

Light can also be used as an artistic medium, whether it has other real purposes or not. Hopefully, *all* site lighting—no matter how serious its purpose—can be developed in an attractive and pleasant decorative manner.

9.2 ACOUSTICS

Controlling sound on sites is somewhat limited, compared to situations inside buildings. Being outdoors results in a general surrounding of existing sound conditions. Although not much can be done to modify or control this situation, site development offers some possible solutions for sound control.

Sound may be generated *on* the site by equipment, traffic, or people; in this case the site planning may take into account the placement of these sound-generating sources, isolating if so desired. For example, the playground of an elementary school may be placed some distance from the library or other spaces requiring quieter conditions. Or, a very noisy piece of outdoor equipment (large fan, etc.) may be situated so as not to disturb a site area intended for rest and relaxation.

Sites may be located near major noise sources, such as airports or busy freeways. If possible, ground forms, high site walls, or tall, dense plantings may be used to reduce some of the noise, but in reality, major sound reduction is limited.

A sound problem may entail privacy in terms of hearing acuity at some location on the site. For example, in developing an outdoor space for a specific activity, the goal may be to either prevent others from hearing what is happening in this space or to have the space protected from other sounds.

Hard design criteria is not extensively available for this work, although some research has been done. Mostly, it is a matter of using common sense and good judgment in terms of planning and placement of various site elements that act as potential sound-separating devices.

Thought should be given to what can be easily achieved in terms of sound management on sites, but it should be understood that there is little potential for protection from boom boxes, motorcycles, rock concerts, etc.

9.3 COMMUNICATION AND SIGNAGE

Communication functions are an aspect of site development. The site facilitates entry and exit to the building, which should be well communicated. This can be accomplished with signs in some cases (see Figure 9.4) or by appropriate placement of sidewalks and driveways.

For large sites with many features or with groups of buildings, there may be resolved communication problems by some combination of site planning

(b)
FIGURE 9.4 Site signs

and signage. For night use this may also involve lighting design—for example, to clearly illuminate both the paths and the signs.

Signs may be developed in an attractive manner, but should above all be readable and noticeable to achieve their basic purposes. The form of many signs, especially those for vehicular traffic management, are often highly controlled by local codes or institutions. The use and effectiveness of warning signs, which carry major safety concerns, should be carefully considered prior to installation.

It is a good design exercise to walk through a proposed site to see how much communication is achieved *without* recourse to signs. If this form of communication is optimal, the signs will work all the better, and will not fight with the visual signals on the site.

9.4 SECURITY

The level of security needed on a site is a function basically of its use and the buildings on it. Security may be a concern because of the site environment, relating to a neighborhood or community condition.

In most situations security is maintained more directly for buildings, with limited concerns for outdoor spaces. However, details of site lighting, landscaping, and placement of site structures may improve the level of security for a building.

Site lighting in general is discussed in Section 9.1. A frequent reason for site lighting is to provide a greater sense of security by relieving the darkness, especially at building entry and exit points and for the traffic paths related to them. This tends to give a comforting feeling to users, and often affords them protection by deterring criminals.

Increased security for a site may be provided with gates, fences, alarms, movement detectors, and surveillance cameras. Where high level security is required, however, these devices are usually supplemented by actual security patrols. Ordinary security may be achieved with some minor adjustments in the design of the facilities, but intense security requires very special considerations.

If enhancement of security is desired, many design decisions are affected. For example, placement of large groups of tall plantings near building entrances or their paths may be rethought to reduce the possibility of their use as hiding places. Choices that might otherwise be made arbitrarily require greater planning so that security is improved.

9.5 BARRIER-FREE SITES

A major factor in site design that has emerged recently is the consideration for the reduction of barriers to persons with limited facilities. These requirements stem from recommendations to actual code requirements, many of which are now state and federal laws. They continue to be defined and redefined, making it critical for site designers to keep abreast of the currently enforceable standards, particularly those with a significant impact on site design decisions and details.

A "barrier" is generally something that prevents access or travel along a path. However, as specified in many situations, it constitutes a general hazard, affecting all users of a facility. Thus, many of the standards now applied in providing access to persons with physical limitations have also generally increased safety for all building users.

Specific requirements, however, result from the specific limitations of the users. Such groups include the following:

Persons using wheelchairs

Elderly persons with limited physical strength

Small children

The vision-impaired, who cannot read signs, see steps, etc.

The hearing impaired, who cannot hear warning buzzers, recorded announcements, etc.

Non-English-speaking persons, who cannot read signs with messages in English

There are many special requirements for each of these groups. However, provisions made for one group often assist others, minimizing the net total of design control factors while affecting a wide range of persons. Special codes apply to many situations, particularly those involving general public usage. However, some of the more general requirements are now incorporated into building codes, no longer designated as relating only to persons with limited capabilities. This is really a matter of extending the range of who we mean when we say "the public." We no longer limit that group only to adults with full hearing, vision, and general agility.

These standards are now becoming widely used in building and site design. Not addressing them in the initial design work may prove to be a costly oversight.

9.6 GENERAL SAFETY CONCERNS

Safety—meaning basically *life safety*—has many dimensions. The bottom line, however, is simply a lack of threat to people in terms of potential injury or death. For building and site design, this applies to considerations for structural load-resistance capacity, fire hazards, dangerous objects in travel paths, electrical shock, exposure to toxic substances, poor lighting, polluted air or water, and anything that appears to be safe but is not. That generally describes the basis for almost everything in the building codes.

While satisfying applicable codes is a means of establishing some level of safety, it should be understood that the nature of the codes is to provide *minimum* requirements. Creating *optimal* conditions means, in almost all situations, going beyond the code requirements. This requires an understanding of the basis of the code requirements: What real problem is being addressed by the code stipulation?

Real life safety is now the focus of attention and a great deal of research and study is being conducted on code requirements and design standards for optimization of safety. While the legally enacted ordinances that create the building codes as enforceable laws are very significant commitments, the informing of designers about real design optimization is a much greater contribution. Optimization factors can be fed into a computer-assisted value analysis to evaluate designs and indicate areas of improvement. Informed design decisions can then be made to help achieve the desired level of the specific performances being considered. This can be done (and frequently is) to reduce costs, but can also affect many other design goals—such as life safety.

10

CASE STUDIES

This chapter presents descriptions of a number of sites whose designs involved various special concerns. Although some good design work is presented, the examples have been chosen primarily to illustrate the design issues and their inherent problems. In most cases, many acceptable solutions are possible, and the readers are challenged to visualize their own ideas to improve the designs.

10.1 PEEKABOO BUILDING

This project consists of a large office building located in a Los Angeles suburb that occupies a valley consisting of rolling hills. If placed in its location and developed as a typical office tower, it would have been about 15 stories high and would have dominated the view for miles around. Since the owner was a prime investor in the development of the suburb, it desired to maintain the general low-rise, residential character of the area and therefore requested a less visible presence.

> Office Building for Prudential Insurance Company; Thousand Oaks, California (35 miles west of central Los Angeles); Albert C. Martin, Los Angeles, architects; (Currently occupied by General Telephone).

As shown in the map sketch in Figure 10.1, the site is bordered by a freeway (the main access to the community) on one side and major streets on two other

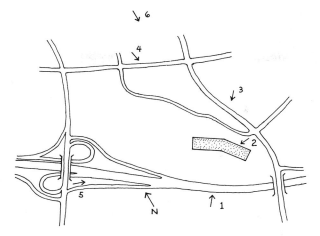

FIGURE 10.1 Map of general area of the Prudential building

sides. The site is quite large, but is almost fully occupied by the building and surface parking lots, except for a wide setback from the freeway. The numbered arrows on the map indicate the positions from which the photos shown in Figures 10.2 through 10.4 were taken.

The building itself consists of a sprawling, three-story structure that makes major use of natural light through horizontal strip windows, interior courts and skylights. The full size of the building can be seen by flying over the property or from some distant hilltops (mostly not occupied), but is otherwise not visually apparent. Plantings, earth berms on two sides, and the general siting of the building conceal it—as well as the considerable site surface parking—from the view of passing motorists or residents in any nearby housing.

The only halfway clear views of the building are from the freeway, as shown in Figure 10.2a, where it can be seen briefly from speeding cars, and from close up on the site, as shown in Figure 10.2*b*. Even in these views, however, the full size of the building is not revealed, so the impact is exceptionally less than that presented by a 15-story tower.

This is a case of using all factors—the existing site features, the building design, and the general site development—to maximize the reduction of the visual impact of a large building with extensive surface parking. The largest trees on the site are giant live oaks, each several hundred years old (the town's namesakes and highly protected for preservation). The rest of the landscape is developed with ground forms and additional plantings that largely preserve the character of the local natural, sea coast arid plain landscape (no palm trees, no rain forest foliage).

Indeed, the building itself has an exterior form that somewhat emulates the soft, rolling hills of the surrounding undeveloped terrain. Not visible here is the selection of exterior finish colors, with brown granite as the major cladding.

(a)

(b)

FIGURE 10.2 General views of the Prudential building: (a) view 1; (b) view 2

Except for the quick view from the freeway, this building is scarcely seen from within the community. The photos in Figure 10.3 illustrate the general views as seen by neighbors and motorists on nearby streets. The only clear views of the building and general site are from aircraft or from some of the surrounding hills. Figure 10.4 shows the view from a hill just north of the property, a view generally experienced only by rabbits and coyotes. Other tall hills, occupied by buildings, are quite a distance from the site.

The site is now somewhat overwhelmed by surrounding development of a much less architecturally stimulating character, and one would wish that this building were actually a bit more visible for the contribution it could make to the generally viewed landscape of the region.

(a)

(b)

(c)

FIGURE 10.3 Views of the Prudential site from nearby streets: (a) view 3; (b) view 4; (c) view 5

FIGURE 10.4 Hilltop view of the Prudential building: view 6

10.2 SITE TRAFFIC JAM

This project consists of a mixed-use facility on the waterfront in downtown Boston. Adjacent to the financial district, it is at the end of a principal street, and one design requirement was to develop the site while preserving a view of the harbor through the site along the axis of the street. With the view as an attraction, the opening as provided also tends to pull pedestrians through the site to the waterfront.

> Rowes Wharf Harbor Redevelopment Project; Boston harbor; Skidmore, Owings, and Merrill, Chicago, architects and engineers.

This is not an exceptionally large facility, but was an important one in the continuing redevelopment of the harbor edge of downtown Boston. The design was the winner in a competition sponsored by the Boston Redevelopment Authority (BRA), which imposed a very complex set of requirements. BRA directed that the project provide:

> Mixed-use development: commercial, residential, retail, maritime.
>
> A major link of the adjacent financial district to the harbor, including the view described previously.
>
> Use of architectural forms and materials in keeping with the character of older buildings in the area.

Stepped down heights of buildings toward the water edge, within a zoning envelope.

Facilitation of a ferry landing currently in operation.

All of this certainly implies a staggerting mix of traffic on the tight site space, bounded on one side by the water and on the opposite side by a nearby elevated freeway. However, as the design developed, it also became necessary to incorporate:

A walk along the water's edge, continuing past the property.

A small marina at the water side of the property.

A health club.

Structure parking on the site for the health club, hotel, office building space, residents of an apartment complex, and patrons of restaurants and retail stores.

Figure 10.5 shows the building and site plan at the street/dockside level and various upper levels. These indicate the general stepped-down form of the building complex, which is actually a series of connected masses. The building section is cut through the largest and tallest portion, parallel to the water front.

Extending over a major portion of the site is an underground structure that contains the health club and parking facility. The construction of this structure (some distance below the water level in the adjacent harbor) resulted in some history-making design work on the parts of the geotechnical and structural consultants and the contractors.

This is literally a totally constructed site, and it had to be integrated with many existing edge conditions. The general building and site designs for this busy complex are exemplary in many ways. The building blends well with existing older buildings as well as with recent redevelopment projects nearby. This non-intrusive presence reads well from a distance, as viewed from boats in the harbor or from passengers in airplanes arriving or taking off at Logan Field, the major airport across the harbor.

At street level, the site generally works well, although it is very difficult to satisfy all possible users. These include persons actually using facilities on the site (several different ones with different hours of peak use), as well as persons strolling along the water's edge or the downtown streets.

The visual and pedestrian link between the harbor and the adjacent downtown area is achieved with a large, arched opening through the tallest structure (see the section in Figure 10.5). The scale of this does not appear massive on the drawing, but is truly impressive when actually viewed. Its presence can even be appreciated from across the harbor, as it is one of a very open view in the mass of buildings along the downtown harbor edge.

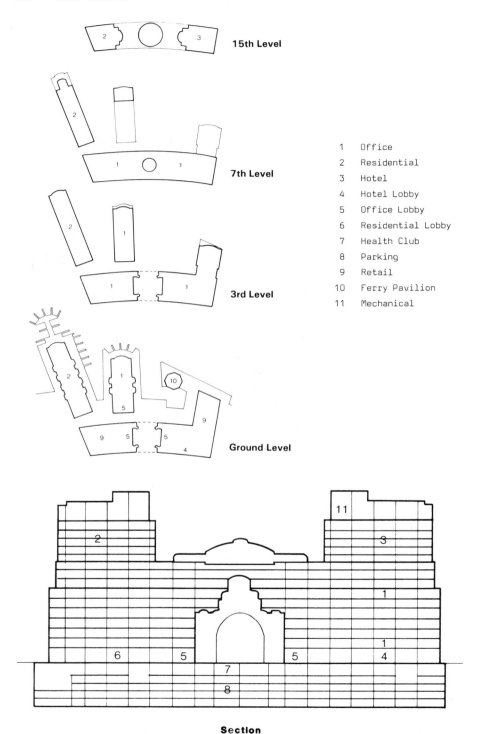

1   Office
2   Residential
3   Hotel
4   Hotel Lobby
5   Office Lobby
6   Residential Lobby
7   Health Club
8   Parking
9   Retail
10 Ferry Pavilion
11 Mechanical

FIGURE 10.5 Section and plans of the Rowes Wharf complex

Vehicular traffic is understandably less casual and potentially enjoyable here, but not more difficult than other such experiences in the typical crowded urban space. Riding in an automobile in Boston is a bit more thrilling than your average rollercoaster ride in a theme park, so the general experience with vehicles here is not to be compared with that at some rural resort area.

This a situation of an almost unimaginable complexity of mixed pedestrian and vehicular traffic: not that unique in many urban areas, but nevertheless a challenging situation for both site and building designers. Urban sites do not often present great opportunities for extensive landscaping development, but typically present difficult work for all the designers and others involved in managing and achieving the construction.

10.3 HELPING THE NEIGHBORS

Occasionally it is possible to develop a property to benefit the developer as well as improve some situation for the neighborhood or community. The examples shown here represent situations in which the construction of a building is executed in a manner that improves the site condition in some significant way.

In this case, the site was a steep cliff between housing at the top and a nearby street at a much lower level. The soil mass of the cliff was slowly eroding, threatening both the housing above and the street below. This was a general problem in the area, with some loss of buildings at the cliff tops, and major disruptions and even rerouting of streets below.

As shown in Figure 10.6, the proposal for this location was to construct some commercial facilities at the edge of the lower street. These buildings would be designed to structurally create giant retaining walls for the cliff, generally stabilizing the precipitous situation for the structures at the cliff edge above.

The photographs in Figure 10.7 show some views of the buildings from

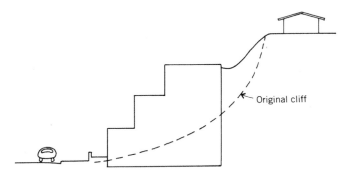

FIGURE 10.6 Site section for the Sunset Boulevard project

(a)

(b)

FIGURE 10.7 Views of the buildings, Sunset Boulevard project

the lower street level. The retaining wall function is not readily visible from this view, except as implied by the stepped-back form of some buildings.

This is a case of making use of a site for buildings considered to be unbuildable. Achieving the site construction without undermining the cliff during the work is a major challenge, adding considerably to the overall project cost. This makes the project, as a commercial or investment project, a special situation, not to be equated with building on a simple, flat site with no problems. The added cost must be covered in some manner, possibly by community subsidy (because the location of the facilities at the lower street is commercially strategic for some reason), help from the property owners at the cliff top, or assistance from government highway agencies (because of the critical need for the lower street).

10.4 THE BUILDING AS A BRIDGE

In many ancient cities buildings were built on bridges, making use of the space in tight urban situations. This is an example of a building built *as* a bridge; it occupies a tight hillside site and spans over a ravine. The ravine is thus left open as a drainage channel and also permits the main access street to the site to go under the building and approach an entrance on the uphill side.

> Pasadena Art Center, Pasadena, California; Craig Ellwood and James Tyler, architects.

This is a situation of using a challenging site without totally destroying its basic form and its generally picturesque quality. The building commands a magnificent view and can itself be viewed well close up from both downhill and uphill positions.

Actually most of the building is not on the bridge, but extends on both sides onto ground planes. (See Figures 10.8 through 10.10.) Nevertheless, the approaching motorist has an excellent view of the building and a quite interesting sequence of experiences in viewing it: from below (downhill side), from underneath (as an impressive span overhead), and from its main entrance level (uphill).

FIGURE 10.8 View of the Design Center from the access street below

FIGURE 10.9 View of the Design Center from the entry level

Unfortunately, the viewer now has the potential to see the building from a much less flattering viewpoint: an uphill parking lot that is above the roof. (See Figure 10.11.) From here it can be observed that the rooftop equipment has not been developed in anything approaching the fine order of the rest of the building. Eventually it is hoped that the growing landscape will help camouflage this somewhat unpleasant viewing experience.

FIGURE 10.10 View of the Design Center from the uphill side

FIGURE 10.11 Roof of the Design Center—a forgettable view

10.5 HUGGING THE HILL

Hillside sites present many possibilities for architectural exploration in terms of buildings and general site development. Buildings are usually quite prominent from downhill viewing positions, and this fact can be used to develop a dramatic, commanding presence. In this example, a deliberately opposite tack was taken, and a major design goal was to make the building an integral part of the hill and void the feel of a dominating presence.

City Services Building for Thousand Oaks, California (35 miles west of Los Angeles); Albert C. Martin Associates, Los Angeles, architects and engineers.

This was a civic government facility for a rapidly growing community developed along a freeway in a high, coastal plane valley. The valley floor consists of many rolling hills and ravines, ringed by a number of low mountain ranges, which present a very soft and pleasant background for viewing the horizon. General development of residential and light commercial construction started by filling the lower regions, but it also crept up the hills in some areas.

The site for this building was some distance up a short hill, with a commanding view of one of the larger flat areas of the valley floor. (See Figure 10.12.) Although it was desired to capitalize on the view and develop a visible presence in the community, it was also desired to keep the building from standing out in the general landscape and to have it blend well with the smaller scale of residential construction.

(See also the building and site in Section 10.1: Same community and architect, although a major corporate client in that case.)

FIGURE 10.12 View of the City Center from across the freeway

The building as developed constitutes a very compatible presence on the hill. Its curved form follows the horizontal section of the rounded hill, and the structure is set partly into the hillside to reduce its protrusion from the hill profile. See Figure 10.13. It is not on top of the hill, but rather a comfortable distance down, permitting the hill to retain its own natural dominant presence in the landscape.

The need for considerable parking was solved by placing some parking on the building roof and the rest in an adjacent, uphill location. (See Figure 10.14.) From a downhill view, the parking is not entirely visible, the building itself being used to screen it from view. As there are no nearby taller hills, the parking is truly only viewed from other hills a considerable distance away.

Landscaping for the site was generally developed with plants compatible with the natural growth in the arid, coastal region of Southern California and

FIGURE 10.13 View of the City Center from the downhill frontage street

FIGURE 10.14 View of the rooftop parking from the unoccupied hill above

those plantings imported by early settlers. This adds to the relatively ''natural'' look of the general site, which also helps to preserve the integrity of the hill.

10.6 CAPPING A HOLE

Many buildings have underground construction that is usually subservient to the major aboveground building. This is a building in which the main activity is underground, and the aboveground building is subservient: it marks the location and functions as an entry and reception area.

> Page Museum at the LaBrea Tar Pits, Los Angeles, California; Thornton, Fagan and Associates, Pasadena, California, architects.

The site for this building is a deep paleontological dig with associated laboratory work and a museum displaying the extensive fossils reclaimed from the dig. The general area is a park, and the building at ground level denotes the location of the museum. The museum is partly at the entry level, but is mostly underground, with ongoing work in the labs on view to visitors.

The site is a park, which protects the property for the dig and the open tar pits, still bubbling gas from surface pools of oil. (See Figure 10.15.) The museum is open to the public, but also houses the ongoing work of the dig. The park grounds house the tar pits and the museum, but also provide a general city park, green space in a densely built-up area of Los Angeles.

The building is developed as a presence in the park, but also appears as what it is—basically the entry to an underground activity. (See Figure 10.16.)

FIGURE 10.15 General site of the LaBrea Tar Pits and park

This is accentuated by the general site development, with the ground sloped up to enclose all but the top of the building on three sides. The "top," in this case, is actually a decorative structure on top of the building's concrete roof slab, which serves as a site sculpture and generally notes the presence of the partly buried building.

FIGURE 10.16 Entry to the Page Museum

This is a case of considerable continuity of the site and building forms, which makes the underground nature of the activity visually apparent. The building is a notable presence, but is clearly subservient to the site and its significance as a park and an historic place.

10.7 EXCITEMENT ON A BORING SITE

This project was developed on what was formerly a large parking lot, an elongated piece of almost dead flat land. The objective was to create a simulated ''natural'' terrain with real earth forms and plants to develop an inward-turning, fantasy land, as an extension of a large theme park. (See Figure 10.17.)

> Snoopy's Camp at Knott's Berry Farm, Buena Park, Anaheim, California; Emmet L. Wemple and Associates, Los Angeles, landscape architects.

This new attraction was developed on part of a large parking lot for the park. This site was literally created from nothing but a plane surface, virtually without any of the usual site features. It was quite an old parking lot, however, and there were several rows of large trees separating the lanes of the parking in part of the lot. These trees were required to be protected and integrated into the design of the new section for the park.

In keeping with the nature of the rest of the park, a continuous walking path through the site was required. The path was to rise and fall gently, cross and recross a simulated stream, be lined with lush foliage, and go past several individual attractions. Development of the contoured site form and the waterways required both cutting down into and building up from the original flat site.

Site edges were mostly closed and developed in a manner to screen views in and out of the site. At points, however, connections had to be made to extensions of existing walks in the park and to existing loops for stagecoach and train rides. The walks and rides were extended through the new site, around and between all of the existing trees.

Because the elongated site was virtually flat, the appearance of a running stream was produced by building the stream in several end-to-end, separate units, with bridges covering the separations from view.

Another important design requirement was a lighting system for night use of the park. This had to provide both general illumination of the site features and patterns related to the walking paths. Much of the lighting is achieved by illuminating site elements, including the plantings, with reflected spill light providing some of the general illumination for pathways. The appearance of an almost daylightlike level of illumination is thus provided without a great number of tall light fixtures.

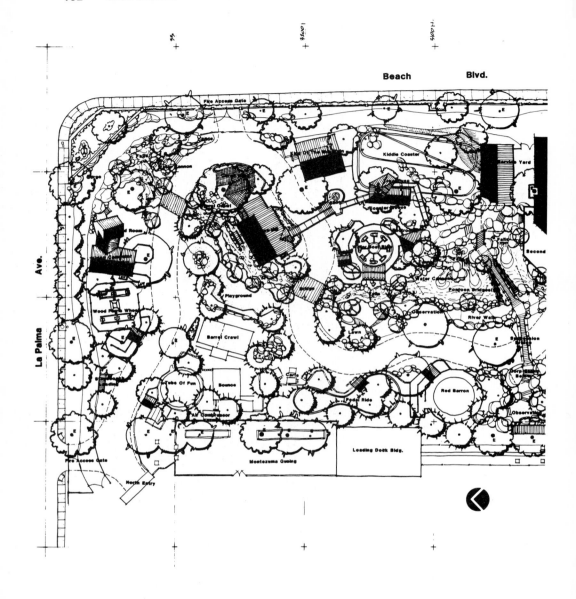

FIGURE 10.17 Landscape plan for Snoopy's Camp

10.8   ALLEVIATING THE WASTELAND

This is a typical situation of a large commercial/industrial facility requiring a considerable amount of parking. The amount of parking and general cost considerations dictate that this be surface parking, if the land is available and is feasible to use in this manner. Because of the high visibility of the property,

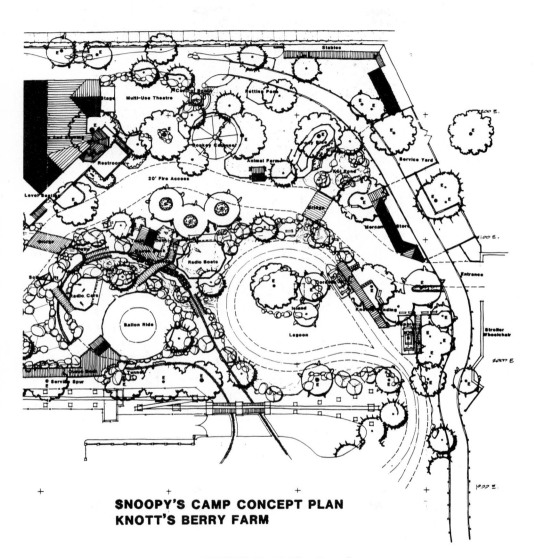

SNOOPY'S CAMP CONCEPT PLAN
KNOTT'S BERRY FARM

FIGURE 10.17 (*Continued*)

the owner in this case decided to invest in additional landscaping and site construction in order to achieve a more attractive site.

Facility for Albuquerque Publishing Company, Albuquerque, New Mexico; Langdon and Wilson, Los Angeles, architects; Emmet L. Wemple and Associates, Los Angeles, landscape architects.

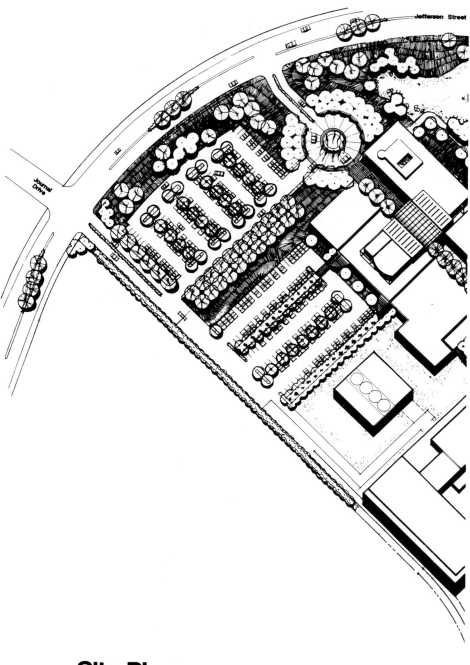

Jefferson Street

Journal Drive

Site Plan

FIGURE 10.18 General landscaping plan for the Albuquerque site

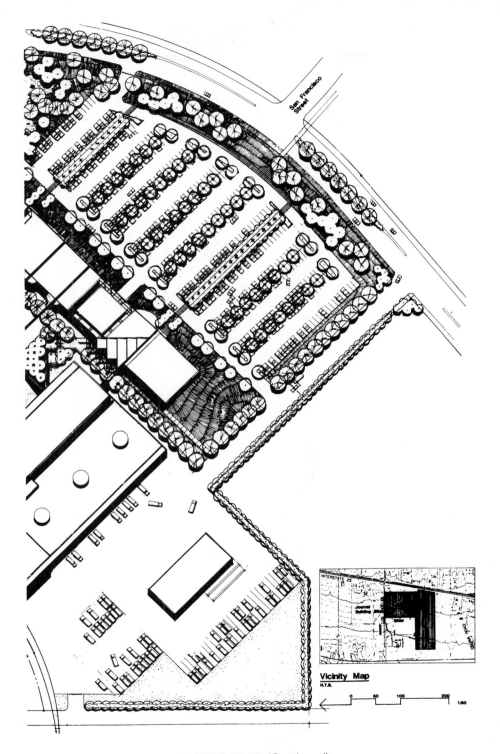

Vicinity Map
N.T.S.

FIGURE 10.18 *(Continued)*

This group of buildings—offices, plant, and warehouse—occupies a large plot of land that is bounded on two sides by a major, curved boulevard. This offers an exceptional amount of visibility from the heavily travelled street. (See Figure 10.18.)

Surface parking was required for four different groups of users:

Visitors
Executives and office employees
Plant and warehouse employees
Trucks and service vehicles

A minimum cost solution would have been to simply blanket the necessary acreage of the flat site with the required amount of asphalt pavement and use curbs, entry gates, fences, and cryptic signs to steer the vehicles to the proper areas. Add a soldierlike lineup of glaring lights on tall poles and you have the typical wasteland of a large parking facility.

The solution here divides the parking into discrete lots, with some placed behind the building to reduce the amount near the street. From the street at any point, from any point on the site, or from inside the buildings, it is not possible to see *all* the parking. The least visible is the truck parking, which is literally out of view of visitors and the general office area and almost fully screened by planting from the street.

A literal forest of trees is also used to achieve other purposes, which include (see Fig. 10.18):

Alleviating the barren pavements of the lots with plantings in the divider strips
Partial screening of individual lots with edge plantings
Partial screening of the entire site from the street
Softening the large mass of buildings with plantings around and between buildings

Plantings are also combined with mounded earth forms to add additional visual interest, and, in some cases, enhance the screening. Within the site, plantings are mostly in neat rows, helping to clarify the identification of separate areas and traffic paths. At the long street edge, however, the land forms and plantings are more randomly developed, avoiding a sterile, militarylike appearance for the property, as viewed from the street.

The layout of the building complex meshes well with the general site development. This is clearly not a case of what is unfortunately common: the landscape architect is called in *after* the buildings have been designed and sited and asked to beautify the site.

10.9 EXPLORING A RAVINE

The example illustrated here represents a proposal for the development of a piece of land within and between existing residential developed areas. The site is a very precipitous ravine; ordinarily what would be considered an unbuildable site. (See Figure 10.19.)

> Proposed Landscape plan for a housing development, Southern California area; Emmet L. Wemple and Associates, Los Angeles, landscape architects.

This site consisted of a picturesque, but precipitous, hillside piece of land, one basically left over when other, more easily developed, areas were built up with housing. A developer proposed to build into the site, while preserving much of it as open ground. The objective was to provide a sufficient number of lots for housing, while retaining an overall appearance of the scenic property as it existed.

A principal concern, as voiced by owners of adjacent, existing houses, was for the loss of the scenic and buffering effects of the existing property, which constituted a green belt of sorts between the highly developed housing areas. To satisfy this concern, the proposal calls for leaving significant parts of the site edges in their natural, existing condition.

The proposed development uses internal streets that follow site contours, and otherwise strives to retain the existing general form and landscape texture of the undeveloped site. Parking areas and housing groups are partly screened with new plantings, and housing groups follow a random layout in keeping with the three-dimensional land form.

For all the efforts of skillful planning, there are some virtually unavoidable problems in this situation. The new housing requires use of access streets in the existing housing and will unavoidably add significant new traffic to these streets. The new mass of residents will also impact somewhat on local facilities: schools, community services, public libraries, etc.

Landscape and architectural planning alone cannot solve all of these problems, and some contention with the neighborhood is likely. This calls for *maximum* use of all the tricks possible to alleviate the problem in a physical and aesthetic design sense, but the social, political, and economic issues will remain. In this case, design was not enough, and the project went down in flames.

It is, nevertheless, an example of almost the best that can be done with the site situation and all the micro-site and macro-site relationships. Assuming that everybody *wanted* the site developed, this is a good proposal.

LEGEND

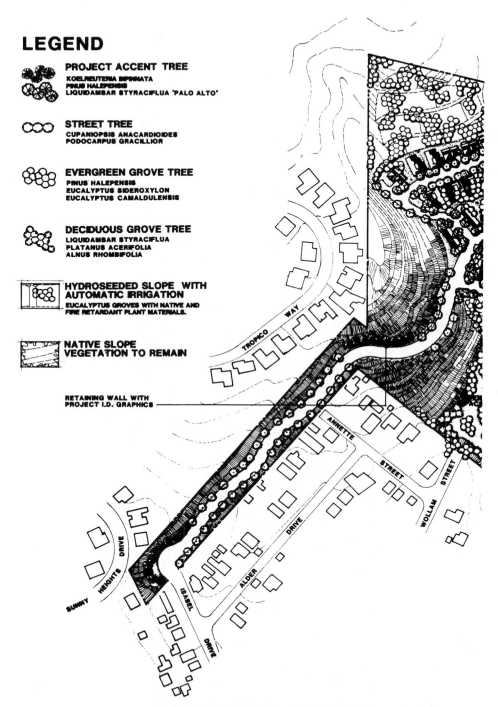

PROJECT ACCENT TREE
KOELREUTERIA BIPINNATA
PINUS HALEPENSIS
LIQUIDAMBAR STYRACIFLUA 'PALO ALTO'

STREET TREE
CUPANIOPSIS ANACARDIOIDES
PODOCARPUS GRACILLIOR

EVERGREEN GROVE TREE
PINUS HALEPENSIS
EUCALYPTUS SIDEROXYLON
EUCALYPTUS CAMALDULENSIS

DECIDUOUS GROVE TREE
LIQUIDAMBAR STYRACIFLUA
PLATANUS ACERIFOLIA
ALNUS RHOMBIFOLIA

HYDROSEEDED SLOPE WITH AUTOMATIC IRRIGATION
EUCALYPTUS GROVES WITH NATIVE AND FIRE RETARDANT PLANT MATERIALS.

NATIVE SLOPE VEGETATION TO REMAIN

RETAINING WALL WITH PROJECT I.D. GRAPHICS

CONCEPTUAL LANDSCAPE PLAN

FIGURE 10.19 Proposed landscape plan for the ravine site

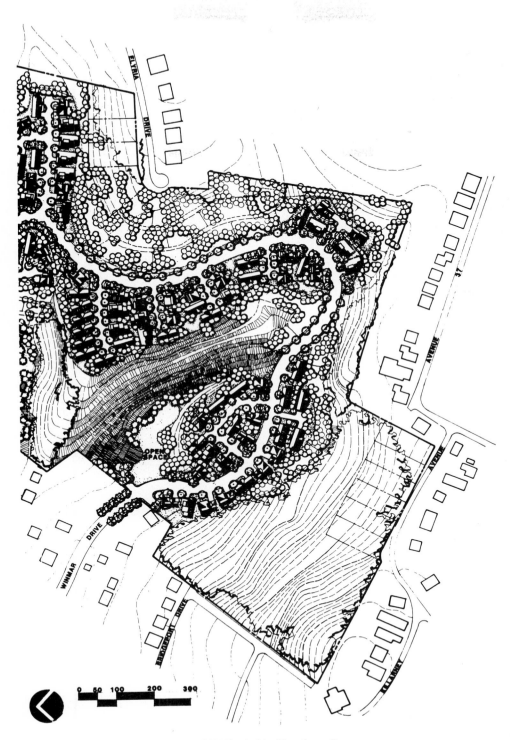

FIGURE 10.19 (*Continued*)

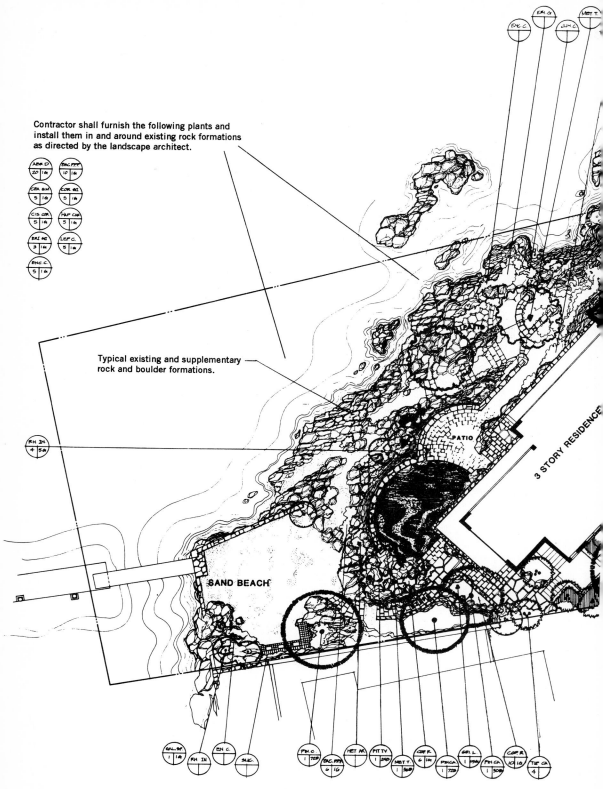

Contractor shall furnish the following plants and install them in and around existing rock formations as directed by the landscape architect.

Typical existing and supplementary rock and boulder formations.

3 STORY RESIDENCE

PATIO

PATIO

SAND BEACH

FIGURE 10.20 Landscape plan for the cliff house

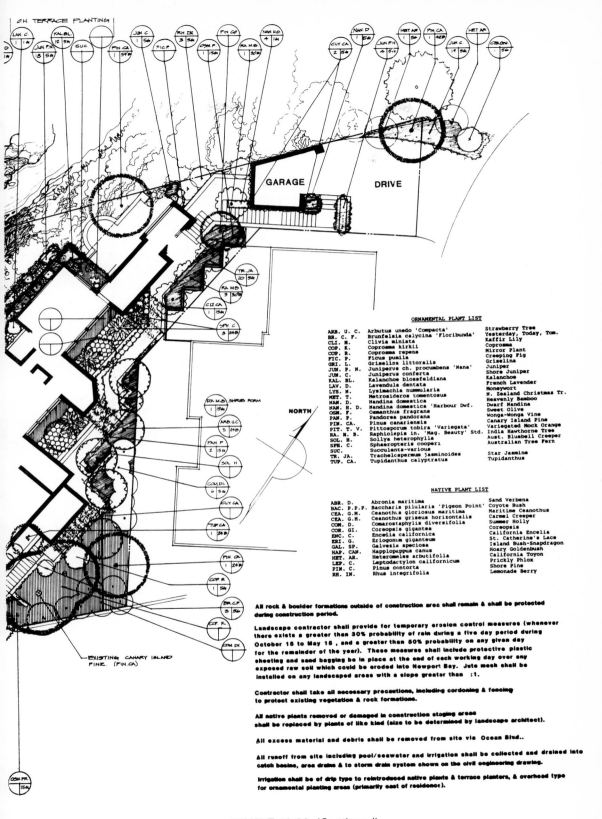

FIGURE 10.20 (Continued)

FIGURE 10.21 View of the cliff house

10.10 SLIPPING INTO A TIGHT SPOT

Sites are sometimes virtually created out of thin air. This is done where development is intense for various reasons. This example is a situation involving very prime beachfront land in Southern California, where ingenuity is continuously at work to squeeze in new, expensive housing.

> Residence, Corona Del Mar, California; Tom Wells, Aspen, Colorado, architect; Emmet L. Wemple and Associates, Los Angeles, landscape architects.

This site is on the ocean front, where rocky cliffs fall almost directly into the water. Existing houses push to the edges of the cliffs, leaving little between them and the water except vertical height separation.

This site was rescued from a cliff with a very minor second ledge. The site is neatly tucked between the water's edge and a house at the cliff edge above. Both horizontal and vertical space is barely adequate to squeeze in the house and keep it reasonably above the largest waves and below the view of the house above. (See Figure 10.20.)

Architectural and landscape designs are tightly woven here, with the house and site developed as a descending staircase to the water's edge from an entry at one tiny end of the site. Considering the lack of site space, the landscape development provides a buffer and a transition between the house and the cliff face at the back of the house, as well as a pleasant transition to the water's edge in front. The house is not actually built *into* the cliff, yet fits it well in a visual sense. (See Figure 10.21.)

11

USE OF COMPUTERS

The use of computers is steadily becoming commonplace in the general working environment of most businesses, design offices included. Beyond word processing, accounting, and other general uses, their employment depends on many factors. This chapter does not present a guide to computer use, but briefly treats the issues involved and some view of present possibilities for use of computers in site design work.

11.1 GENERAL CONSIDERATIONS: HARD AND SOFT

There is, at any given time, a considerable array of computer equipment, software programs, and documentation available for use in design work. Obtaining it and using it present various considerations, as follows:

Economics. Not much is free. Getting it, learning how to use it, and operating it for productive purposes is expensive.

Awareness. Finding out what is available, what is really useful for your purposes, and what the relative value of competing products is can be a real challenge for the experienced user, let alone the beginner.

In general, it is advisable to utilize independent sources (not vendors or manufacturers) to research what is useful and which products are available and competitive on the market. Some feedback of user experience is also desirable. This field is full of hype—some very sincere, but mostly overwhelming to the inexperienced.

A first consideration in this should be some perceived needs. You need to have a firm grip on what you are doing or want to do to know how the computer can help. The rest of this chapter deals with some basic tasks of design offices and what computers can presently do to help. Think these things through before talking to sales people.

A major problem used to be simply learning how to use computers. With a combination of more user-friendly equipment and software on the one hand and better instructional sources on the other, this is now not much of a problem. Still, if you start from scratch, count on going to school to learn the basics; self-instruction is almost nonexistent here.

11.2 GENERAL DATA CRUNCHING

A basic task that computers can handle well is that of processing large masses of information. Storing data in compact form is an advantage, but the real plus is the ability to access it, analyze it, and deliver it for use in a specific programmed operation. The real advantage of this capability depends on the needs of the user. For design firms this generally means some basic tasks, such as performing investigations, testing proposed design schemes, making drawings, writing specifications, and analyzing of the final design.

The next two sections of this chapter treat two primary tasks that are especially useful in site design: making drawings and performing analyses of site conditions, both existing and proposed. Both of these tasks involve considerable time and effort when performed by ''hand'' processes. Some efficiency can be developed with good management, but for really large or complex problems the task remains laborious.

Once an office computer system is in place, it can usually be directly utilized, or relatively easily expanded, to perform various tasks. Unless it is already working to capacity, a system set up primarily for word processing may be used to perform data handling or other work. The expansion necessary may relate to the hardware (equipment), software (programs and documents), personnel (computer wranglers); or, possibly, to all factors.

A data-handling system that operates to process information directly in the office can also be easily used to import data from large external data sources (over phone lines). This is of major importance for some types of site analyses involving existing weather data, long-term cyclic effects, extensive geological studies, and the imaging, analyzing, and possibly printing out of complex forms for graphic or model studies.

The super data-cruncher is handy to have for its time- and space-saving features, but its real worth for a design office is the creation of some design investigation capabilities that are simply otherwise not feasible. This may have to do with the time available for the design work. Design work must progress to some output (the designed object), and if all the available time is used up for extensive investigation, the designer will be well informed but basically empty handed.

11.3 COMPUTER-GENERATED DRAWINGS

Drawings—mostly black line on white paper—are still the primary media for recording and transmitting information of design work, and for defining the final design work. However, they are also used extensively for studies throughout the design process. Quite often, elements appearing on the final drawings will have been drawn many times during the design development, when ideas are being explored, alternatives proposed and tested, and the final scheme progressively tuned and fitted to achieve the final form.

During the design process, there are typically many people that must be informed of the progress of the design work. This includes other members of the design team (often working on related parts of the work), outside consultants, the design client, and various people with interest and possibly approval functions.

The paper flow alone can decimate whole forests, let alone utilize countless hours of work generating the drawings. Computer-generated graphics have the potential to reduce time, effort, storage problems, and the transmission activity for this kind of information. Images of drawings can be generated in the computer and sent to a printout device; or they can be endlessly modified in the computer, letting the computer screen substitute for many copies of preliminary drawings. And they can be transmitted to others, also working on computers anywhere in the world (connected by cable or phone) without the necessity of a print being made.

This fairy tale of automation will be slickly described for you by any number of companies or vendors, using 3D images, animation, and full sound accompaniment. You can buy their whole package of equipment, priority software, training programs, lifetime service, and general all around mothering. And spend the next several years trying to pay for it while figuring out how to make it work for you.

Other than the financing for such an operation, the biggest problem in implementing it is the conversion of designers from pen on paper to image on-screen graphics. Most designers now working were trained basically as hand drafters or sketch artists in graphics work. If they have any developed skills in this area, they are probably paper bound. Training can be achieved, but it must often flow from this background.

Large, complex graphics use up a lot of computer capacity and require some expensive equipment for high quality, large size printouts. Since the design and construction fields still use large drawings as a basic medium of information exchange, this remains a problem of concern. Eventually, greater use will be made of other methods of recording and exchanging information, and architects, engineers, and other designers will join the rest of the world in using the universal 8.5 × 11 in. format. But for now, the making of the large drawings (formerly on large drafting boards) is still a necessity.

The whole computer industry moves rapidly in development of new, more competitive, products. This works generally to make both equipment and software less expensive, smaller, more functional, easier to use, and steadily more accessible to smaller and smaller end users. In fact, the small design office may be a principal winner in this as the ability to perform more complex and demanding work becomes feasible with less and less in terms of space, equipment, and staff size.

11.4 COMPUTER-AIDED INVESTIGATIONS AND ANALYSES

Designers are used to handling information, but they are not thrilled by the process and effort required to obtain and analyze it. Anything that helps to simplify and speed up these tasks is welcomed.

Investigations produce raw data. For any useful design applications, the data must usually be analyzed for its relative significance to the design problems. Raw data or results of analyses may be fed into design programs to produce some actual design results. Value analyses can be made of the design solutions to yield some data for comparative evaluations of alternate solutions.

This is the process of informed design. The greater the mass of information and the more relationships it affects, the more the computer can help. The more rational the design process, the more likely it can be stated in computer language and supported by the computer. For many design tasks, this can result in some real shortcuts from raw data to design solutions.

Most site design problems have a limited set of predictable alternative solutions. Various properties of the alternatives can be compared with the requirements derived from the analysis of problem data. Presto! The automated design solution. Or at least, some ranked order of the alternatives in regard to some specific value: cost, safety, time to achieve, toxic pollution generated, noise created, etc.

In the range of design issues from purely functional to purely aesthetic, these automated, rational processes obviously help most on the functional end. To the extent that those types of issues are predominant or simply excessive in number, design work yields highly to being computer-assisted.

11.5 MISCELLANEOUS PROBLEMS

Working computers into an existing design operation typically presents a number of general considerations. The following are two issues that must be addressed in this regard.

1. To what extent, and in what significant ways, are the design tasks in the field subject to reasonably rational analysis?

Response to this question generally favors situations in which value judgments concerning effective design are essentially in functional terms. The more subjective the judgment, the less the potential for clean, rational evaluation. Thus, we can be quite rational about the selection of the chemistry for a paint for a specific application, but not so rational about whether the color is "right."

2. Is there an existing inventory of computer materials for use in a particular design field?

This generally depends on two basic considerations. First, are there enough people likely to use the necessary equipment and software to justify their development, production, and marketing? Second, is there anybody capable of developing the designs for the necessary equipment and software?

Regarding the first question, it is a relatively simple matter to add up a body count for any particular job. How many people are there trying to write letters, reports, directives, etc., at a given time? The answer: a lot. Consequently, the equipment and programs for simple word processing are numerous, highly competitively priced, and readily available. On the other hand, there are really not so many people trying to do site planning, so IBM and others are not enormously concerned about supporting the work.

The second question is more insidious. The people who design computer equipment or develop computer programs may be super geniuses in those tasks, but they are very likely not experienced in the design fields for which they design the equipment or software. Thus, the computer support may not actually be applied to the really critical design judgments and tasks, and the designer is not really assisted in the most significant aspects of the design work.

All of this generally improves over time; where attempts have been in progress for a long time, the support is more likely to be effective, available, and extensive. Where the interest, concern, and participation has been only recently developed, you can expect less accomplishment. People in fields of science and engineering began experimenting with computers when they first emerged and have steadily been the first eager users of the leading edge technology. More recently, people in banking and investments have caught on. Architects, landscape architects, and interior designers are quite late on the scene.

11.6 SOFTWARE AND DESIGN AID SOURCES

There is a considerable array of available equipment to support computer-aided design work. It is quite difficult to assess the inventory at any given time, but it is there, accompanied by an equal amount of information. Assuming you can select, obtain, and afford the necessary equipment, the problem remains of using it. This is the greater problem in operational terms. Operating software, training programs, and user support are the major areas for future development.

The primary need is not for the involvement of more computer experts, but for the participation of more educators and working professionals. Where this participation exists, it is usually a knowledgeable, impartial source of information, (unrelated to selling products). For beginners, this help is invaluable in reducing the vulnerability to aggressive marketers of products.

Product information obtained directly from vendors or producers is essential and useful, but its objectivity is obviously to be questioned. Collect all the information you can, but don't try to analyze it without help from more experienced people with nothing to sell.

REFERENCES

1. H. Rubenstein, *A Guide to Site and Environmental Planning*, 3rd, ed., Wiley, New York, 1987.
2. J. Roberts, *The Building Site: Planning and Practice*, Wiley, New York, 1983.
3. K. Lynch and G. Hack, *Site Planning*, 3rd ed., MIT Press, Cambridge, MA, 1988.
4. T. Walker, *Site Design and Construction Detailing*, 2nd ed., PDA Publications, Mesa, AZ, 1986.
5. J. DeChiara and L. Koppelman, *Time-Saver Standards for Site Planning*, McGraw-Hill, New York, 1984.
6. C. Harris and N. Dines, *Time-Saver Standards for Landscape Architecture*, McGraw-Hill, New York, 1988.
7. R. Austin, T. Dunbar, J. Hulverson, and K. Todd, *Graphic Standards for Landscape Architecture*, Van Nostrand Reinhold, New York, 1986.
8. G. Jameson and M. Verson, *Site Details*, Van Nostrand Reinhold, New York, 1989.
9. C. Ramsey and H. Sleeper, *Architectural Graphic Standards*, 8th ed., Wiley, New York, 1988.
10. H. Parker and J. MacGuire, *Simplified Site Engineering for Architects and Builders*, 2nd ed., Wiley, New York, 1991.
11. J. Ambrose, *Simplified Design of Building Foundations*, 2nd ed., New York, Wiley, 1988.
12. *Uniform Building Code*, 1988 ed., International Conference of Building Officials, Whittier, CA.

13. J. Ambrose, *Building Construction: Site and Below-Grade Systems*, Van Nostrand Reinhold, New York, 1991.

14. F. Merritt, *Standard Handbook for Civil Engineers*, 3rd ed., McGraw-Hill, New York, 1983.

15. B. Kavanagh and S. J. Bird, *Surveying-Principles and Applications*, 2nd ed., Prentice-Hall, Englewood Cliffs, NJ, 1989.

16. *Sweet's Catalog File: Products for General Building and Renovation*, issued annually, Sweet's Division, McGraw-Hill Information Systems Co., New York.

GLOSSARY

The material presented here consists of a dictionary of the major words and terms from the field of site engineering that are used in the work in this book. For fuller explanation of most entries, the reader should use the Index to find the related discussions in the text.

Access. The ability to get to, onto, or into something; usually refers to the ability to get into a site or building on the site. Barrier-free access refers to access by persions with limited capacities, typically persons in wheelchairs.

Acoustics. Sound performance characteristics.

Architect. Professional person whose basic service is the design of buildings.

Asphalt. A bituminous material (oil-based); usually refers to concrete made with sand, gravel, and a bituminous binder (as used for pavements).

Backfill. See Fill.

Barrier-free access. See Access.

Benchmark. Permanent point of known and recorded elevation.

Building base. The bottom of a building, including its foundations.

Building code. Set of regulations affecting building design and construction.

Building footprint. The outline of a horizontal section (plan) of the building, usually at the ground plane.

Building permit. Document of approval for construction, issued by authorities having jurisdiction of approval.

Building services. Services supplied to buildings, such as electric power, water, gas, sewers, etc.

Building site. The property on which a building is constructed.

Building/site relations. The interactive relationships between a building and the site it occupies.

Cantilever retaining wall. See Retaining wall.

Cartography. Making of maps.

Catch basin. Water-holding device (well, tank, etc.) used to intercept water before it enters a sewer.

Channel. A device for concentrating flowing surface water.

Channelling. The process of collecting flowing surface water into concentrated streams.

Civil engineer. Professional person with engineering specialization in the various branches of civil engineering (highways, site engineering, structures, water control, etc.).

Compaction. Action that tends to lower the void ratio and increase the density of a soil mass; generally refers to squeezing it into its least volume.

Construction plan. Plan of a building or site showing the position, form, dimensions, and other data for proposed construction.

Contour. Line on a map connecting points of the same elevation (vertical height).

Contour interval. Difference in height of adjacent contour lines on a map.

Curb. Edging device that achieves a small change in elevation; essentially a very short retaining wall.

Cut. Reduction of the surface of a site below original grade level. See Fill.

Datum. The reference level (horizontal plane) to which point elevations or contours are related, usually mean sea level.

Design problem. The statement of what needs to be designed and what constraints exist to influence design development.

Drilled-in anchor. Anchoring device seated in rock or very dense soil; installed by drilling into the seating mass.

Easement. A legal claim on some rights regarding a piece of property, such as the right to place transmission wiring overhead, extend a public thoroughfare, or install a sewer line.

Elevation. Vertical distance from a datum plane (horizontal reference plane). See Datum.

Erosion. Progressive loss of a soil mass, usually by flowing water.

Excavation. Cut below the existing grade of a site for purposes of construction.

Fill. 1. Buildup of the site surface above the original grade. See Cut. 2. Soil deposit produced by other than natural effects. Backfill is soil deposited in the excessive part of an excavation after completion of construction in the excavation.

Finished grade. See Grade.

Footing. A pad, usually of concrete, used to spread a load onto the ground surface; usually placed some distance below the finished grade.

Framed pavement. A pavement surface produced as the top of a framed structure, usually concrete.

Geotechnical consultant. Professional person with expertise in soils engineering, geology, etc.

Geotechnical survey. Investigation of a site relating to various concerns for soil materials, behaviors, and potential problems.

Geotextile. A synthetic fabric; various forms used in construction with soils for various purposes.

Grade. 1. Elevation of the ground surface at some location; often qualified as *original* grade, *finished* (re-established) grade, etc. 2. Slope of the ground surface (angle from the horizontal) at some location, also called Gradient or Slope.

Gradient. See Grade.

Grading. Site work consisting of redevelopment of the form of the ground surface.

Gravity retaining wall. See Retaining wall.

Ground cover. Anything besides soil used to produce a site surface; usually refers to surface-spreading plants, such as grass or ivy.

Handicapped parking. Commonly used (but demeaning) term for parking stalls intended to facilitate persons who enter or leave a car from a wheelchair.

Illumination. The light on an object or the amount of light falling on a given point. General illumination refers to the overall lighting of a large area or space. Task lighting refers to the illumination provided for a specific task, such as walking down a stair, reading a sign, etc.

Interpolation. Establishment of a numerical value by linear proportionality between two sequential numbers. Example: finding the elevation of a point by using the adjacent contour elevations and the distances of the point from the contour lines.

Invert. Elevation of the lowest part of the inside of a pipe or tunnel.

Invisible site. The portion of a site that is below the site surface; typically contains foundations, roots of plants, service piping and wiring, etc.

Irrigation. Water for plant cultivation, supplied by artificial means (not rain).

Lagging. Boards or timbers used to develop a surface to retain the vertical cut face of an excavation.

Land surveyor. Professional person who performs various tasks, including the preparation of site surveys.

Landscape architect. Professional person with primary responsibilities for general site design.

Landscaping. The work of developing the finished, mostly decorative completion of site work.

Laying out. Refers to establishing the location for some object, such as a foundation or roadway.

Layout. The graphic display (plan, site map, etc.) of the arrangement of some object or objects.

Level. 1. Horizontally flat (zero slope). 2. Elevation (height above a datum plane). 3. Instrument for reading angles in a horizontal plane.

Levelling. The process of determining the difference in elevation between two points, usually by using a Level and a Levelling rod.

Levelling rod. Rod with accurate graduation markings, used with a Level to perform Levelling.

Life safety. See Safety.

Loose-laid retaining wall. See Retaining wall.

Macro-site. The world outside the site edges.

Micro-site. The world inside the site edges.

Minimal. Qualification as barely adequate or least acceptable.

Optimal. Qualification as the most favorable or the most that can be expected for a given situation.

Overturning effect. The toppling or tipping over effect of lateral forces.

Parking lot. Site area assigned to parking and associated drives.

Parking stall. Area assigned to a single vehicle for parking.

Pavement. Structural surfacing of the ground for walks, drives, parking lots, etc.

Pavement base. The underlying support for a structural pavement; typically prepared as such in some ways.

Paver. Single, separate unit used to develop a pavement surface; may be loose-laid or set in mortar.

Plane surveying. Surveying that assumes the surface of the earth in a relatively small region to be flat.

Planimeter. Instrument used for measuring the area of plane figures.

Planner. One who makes plans; generally used to described a professional person whose field is in the **macro-site**, that is, in urban, community, or regional planning.

Planter. A container for growing plants; may simply be a plot of ground with edging, but usually describes a structure, either freestanding or built into the ground.

Plantings. A set of growing plants used to develop the landscaping for a site.

Plot. A piece of land (site) defined by established boundaries.

Plot plan. A maplike plan of a plot (site), generally showing the existing conditions; may be a simplified version of the site survey.

Property line. Line on a site survey or plot plan indicating the boundary of the property.

Raker. A diagonal compression brace (strut) used to stabilize an element as part of the bracing for a vertical cut face in an excavation; also called a *kicker*.

Recontouring. Manipulation of the existing contours on a plot (site) plan as part of the design for regrading the site surface.

Regrading. The construction work of moving surface soils to develop a re-contoured form for a site.

Runoff. Water flowing from a surface during precipitation (rain).

Safety. Condition of being relatively free from potential harm; relating to some specific harmful effect, such as that due to structural collapse, fire, explosion, etc; now more specifically described as **life safety**, referring to human life.

Security. Condition of being protected; in site and building design, refers mostly to protection from intrusion of unwelcome visitors (burglars, etc.).

Sewer. The system for collection, removal, and disposal of waste water and water-borne wastes.

Shear key in footing. Downward protruding ridge on the bottom of a footing to help with resistance to sliding.

Sheet piling. Sheet-form steel elements, generally with pleated and inter-locking cross sections, driven into soil to form a vertical wall.

Site. A specific point or small region on the surface of the earth.

Site construction. General description of the man-made site, consisting of constructed elements (pavements, walls, etc.) and the recontoured soils; also frequently used to refer only to the constructed elements.

Site design. The general activity of developing plans for a constructed site; incorporates all issues relating to the site and typically involves or overlaps the work of many professionals.

Site development. The work of constructing a site in compliance with design plans.

Site edges. The sides (property lines, etc.) of a site in plan; usually also refers to the conditions beyond the sides and outside the property.

Site planning. The general arranging of the site surface and the various items on it.

Site survey. Map of a site, usually prepared by a *land surveyor*, showing data pertaining to the legal definition of the site and various aspects of physical site features.

Siting a building. Locating a building on its construction site.

Slab on grade. A concrete paving slab, cast directly on the ground (usually on a prepared pavement base).

Slope. The vertical angle between the horizontal and some portion of the ground surface in a particular direction. See also Grade.

Slope angle limit. Limit for the angle from the horizontal of the sloping face of a soil mass; described as the *safe limit*, if stability is generally not a problem; described as the *failure limit*, if slipping failure is imminent.

Soldier beam. Vertical element (sometimes a driven pile) used with horizontal sheet or plank elements (lagging) to provide bracing for the vertical cut sides of a deep excavation.

Spot elevation. Height (elevation; vertical distance) of a point on the ground surface with respect to a datum plane.

Stability of a slope. Relative likelihood for a sloping ground surface to remain in place against the effects of erosion or slippage of the soil mass.

Staking out. Process of using stakes driven into the ground surface of a site to locate the position of some construction work.

Structure parking. Parking developed within a structure; may be inside a building or in a separate structure developed primarily for the parking.

Surface parking. Parking developed on a site surface; usually with some form of pavement.

Survey. 1. General: to observe and note facts about something, such as the general features of a site. 2. To perform surveying work (levelling, etc.). 3. The documentation of surveying work for a site.

Surveying. The work of using instruments to measure or locate features on a site, such as the elevation of a point on the surface, position of the property lines, etc.

Task lighting. See Illumination.

Title. The recorded ownership of something or the actual document that establishes the ownership.

Topology. A study of the accurate description (topology) of a place.

Traffic path. The portion of a site surface dedicated to the achievement of some travel, typically either as a footpath for pedestrians or a driveway for vehicles.

Transit. Surveying instrument for measuring both horizontal and vertical angles. See Level.

Tunnel. An underground, tubular construction, as a channel for the flow of something: people, trains, utility services, waste water, etc.

Visible site. The *viewed site*, consisting of the site surface and the objects on it.

Watershed. The area drained by a drainage device (channel, downspout, area drain, etc.).

Zoning ordinance. A legally enforceable description of limitations affecting usage of some portion of a political jurisdiction (city, county, etc.).

SOIL PROPERTIES AND USAGE CONSIDERATIONS

Undoubtedly, the major "element" in site construction is the site itself, as constituted by the soils that define its surface and immediate subsurface layers. Transforming a site into a constructed object means working extensively with the site soils. This is a significant aspect of foundation design, pavement design, landscape design, and general site design.

Besides providing support or encasement for various objects, soils are also frequently used for some forms of direct construction. Although topsoil, plantings, paving, or various ground covers may be used to develop surfaces, the general surface is usually developed by the underlying soils. Achieving this general site "construction" consists of treating the soils as construction materials. This view is necessary in order to understand the structural character and limitations of soils.

In landscaping development it is also necessary to understand the nature of soil as it relates to establishing and nurturing plantings. Where extensive planting is to be developed, an early issue to be settled is the potential of using existing site materials and the necessary means of preserving them for final landscaping work.

The materials in this appendix present a general summary of soil concerns regarding the surface and subsurface ground masses of most sites. This material has been abstracted from various references, but mostly from *Simplified Design of Building Foundations* (Ref. 11).

Information about the materials that constitute the earth's surface is forthcoming from a number of sources. Persons and agencies involved in fields such as agriculture, landscaping, highway and airport paving, waterway and dam construction, and the basic earth sciences of geology, mineralogy, and hydrology have generated research and experience that is useful to those involved in general site development.

A.1   SOIL CONSIDERATIONS RELATED TO SITE DEVELOPMENT

Some fundamental properties and behaviors of soils related to site development concern are described in this section.

Soil Strength.   For bearing-type foundations a major concern is the soil resistance to vertical compression. Resistance to horizontal pressure and sliding friction are also of concern in situations involving the lateral (horizontally directed) effects due to wind, earthquakes, or retained soil.

Dimensional Stability.   Soil volumes are subject to change, the principal sources being changes in stress or water content. This affects settlement of foundations and pavements, swelling or shrinking of graded surfaces, and general movements of site structures.

General Relative Stability.   Frost actions, seismic shock, organic decomposition, and disturbance during site work can also produce changes in the physical conditions of soils. The degree of soil sensitivity to these actions is called their relative stability. Highly sensitive soils may require modification as part of the site development work.

Uniformity of Soil Materials.   Soil masses typically occur in horizontally stratified layers. Individual layers vary in their composition and thickness. Conditions can also vary considerably at different locations on a site. A major early investigation that must precede any serious engineering design is that of soil profiles and the properties of individual soil components at the site. Depending on the site itself and the nature of the work proposed for the site, this investigation may proceed to considerable depth below grade.

Groundwater Conditions.   Various conditions, including local climate, proximity to large bodies of water, and the relative porosity (water penetration resistance) of soil layers, affect the presence of water in soils. Water conditions may affect soil stability, but also relate to soil drainage, excavation problems, need for irrigation, etc.

Sustaining Plant Growth.   Where site development involves considerable new planting, the ability of surface soils to sustain plant growth and respond to irrigation systems must be considered. Existing surface soils must often be modified or replaced to provide the necessary conditions.

The discussions that follow present various issues and relationships that affect these and other concerns for site development.

A.2 GROUND MATERIALS

Various materials compose the natural or generally nonconstructed surface of the earth. This section treats the most common materials.

Soil and Rock.   The two basic solid materials that constitute the earth's crust are soil and rock. At the extreme, the distinction between the two is clear: for example, loose sand versus solid granite. However, a precise division is somewhat more difficult, since highly compressed soils may be quite hard, and some types of rock are quite soft or contain many fractures, making them relatively susceptible to disintegration. For practical use in engineering, soil is generally defined as any material consisting of discrete particles that are relatively easy to separate, while rock is any material that requires considerable brute force for its excavation.

Fill.   In general, fill is material that has been deposited on the site to build up the ground surface. Many naturally occurring soil deposits are of this nature, but for engineering purposes, the term fill is mostly used to describe *man-made fill* or other deposits of fairly recent origin. The issue of concern for fill is primarily its recent origin and the lack of stability that this represents. Continuing consolidation, decomposition, and other changes are likely. The uppermost soil materials on a site are likely to have the character of fill, man-made or otherwise.

Organic Materials.   Organic materials near the ground surface occur mostly as partially decayed plant materials. These are highly useful in sustaining new plant growth, but generally represent undesirable stability conditions for various engineering purposes. Organically rich surface soils (*topsoil*) are a valuable resource for landscaping, and indeed may have to be imported to the site when they do not exist in sufficient amounts. For support of pavements, site structures, or building foundations, however, they are generally undesirable.

Investigation of site conditions is done partly to determine the general inventory of these and other existing materials, with a view toward the general management of the site materials in the intended site development. Critical concerns for this management are discussed in Section 4.6.

A.3 SOIL PROPERTIES AND IDENTIFICATION

The following material deals with various soil properties and their significance in the identification of soils and determination of their behaviors.

Soil Composition

A typical soil mass is visualized as consisting of three parts, as shown in Figure A.1. The total soil volume comprises solid particles and the open spaces

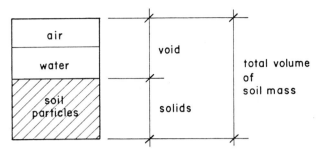

FIGURE A.1 Three-part composition of a soil mass

between the particles, called the *void*. The void space is typically filled by some combination of gas (usually air) and liquid (usually water). There are several soil properties that relate to this composition, such as the following.

Soil Weight. Most of the materials that constitute the solid particles in ordinary soils have a unit density that falls within a narrow range. Expressed as specific gravity (the ratio of the unit density to that of water), the range is from 2.6 to 2.75, or from about 160 to 170 lb/cu. ft. Sands typically average about 2.65, clays about 2.70. Notable exceptions are soils containing large amounts of organic (mostly plant) materials. If the unit weight of a dry soil sample is determined, the amount of void can thus be closely approximated.

Void Ratio. The amount of soil void can be expressed as a percentage of the total volume. However, in engineering work, the void is usually expressed as the ratio of the volume of the void to that of the solid. Thus, a soil with 40% void would be said to have a void ratio of 40/60, 0.67. Either means of expression can be used for various computations of soil properties.

Porosity. The actual percentage of void is expressed as the porosity of the soil, which in coarse-grained soils (sand and gravel) is generally an indication of the rate at which water flows through or drains from the soil. The actual water flow is determined by standard tests, however, and is described as the relative *permeability* of the soil.

Water Content. The amount of water in a soil sample can be expressed in two ways: by the *water content* and by the *saturation*. They are defined as follows:

$$\text{Water Content} = (\text{weight of water/weight of solids})(100)$$
$$\text{Saturation} = \text{volume of water/volume of void}$$

Full saturation occurs when the void is totally filled with water. Oversaturation is possible when the water literally floats or suspends the solid particles, increasing the void. Muddy water is really very oversaturated soil.

Size and Gradation of Soil Particles

The size of the discrete particles that constitute the solids in a soil is significant in identifying the soil and evaluating its physical characteristics. Since most soil deposits have a wide range of sizes (expressed as the size *gradation*), full identification of a soil requires determining the precentages of particles of particular size categories.

The two common means of measuring grain size are by sieve and sedimentation. The sieve method consists of passing the pulverized dry soil sample through a series of sieves of increasingly smaller openings. The percentage of the total original sample that is retained on each sieve is recorded. The finest sieve is a No. 200, with openings of approximately 0.003 in.

A broad distinction is made between the total amount of solid particles that passes the No. 200 sieve and those retained on all the sieves. Those passing the No. 200 sieve are called the *fines*, and the total retained is called the *coarse fraction*.

The fine-grained soil particles are further subjected to a *sedimentation test*. This consists of placing the dry soil in a sealed container with water, shaking the container, and measuring the rate of settlement of the particles. The coarser particles will settle in a few minutes; the finest may take several days.

Figure A.2 shows a graph used to record grain size characteristics of soils. The horizontal scale uses a log scale since grain size range is quite extensive. Some common soil names, based on grain size, are given at the top of the graph. These are approximations since some overlap occurs at the boundaries, particularly for the fine-grained materials. The distinction between sand and gravel is specifically established by the No. 4 sieve, although the actual materials that constitute the coarse fraction are often the same across the grain size range.

The curves shown on the graph in Figure A.2 are representative of some particularly characteristic soils, described as follows:

A *well-graded* soil consists of some significant percentages of a wide range of soil particle sizes.

A *uniform* soil has a major portion of its particles grouped in a small size range.

A *gap-graded* soil has a wide range of sizes, but with some concentrations of single sizes and small percentages over some ranges.

Shape of Soil Particles

The shape of soil particles is also significant for some soil properties. The three major classes of shape are bulky, flaky, and needlelike, the latter being quite rare. Sand and gravel are typically bulky, with a further distinction being made as to the degree of roundness of the particle shape, ranging from angular to well rounded.

Bulky-grained soils are usually quite strong in resisting static loads, especially when the grain shape is quite angular, as opposed to well rounded. Unless a bulky-grained soil is well graded or contains some significant amount

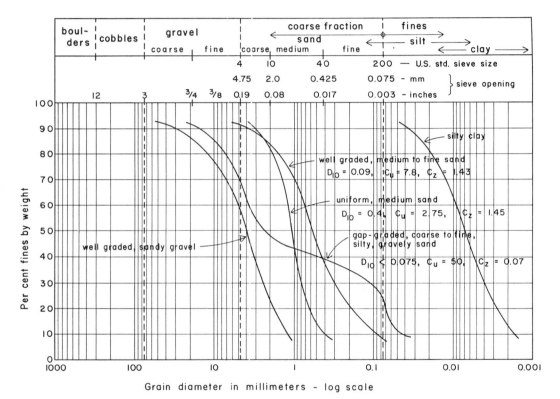

FIGURE A.2 Grain size range for soils

of fine-grained material, however, it can be subjected to displacement and consolidation (reduction in volume) due to shock or vibration.

Flaky-grained soils tend to be easily deformable or highly compressible, similar to the action of randomly thrown, loose sheets of paper or dry leaves in a container. A relatively small percentage of flaky-grained particles can create the character of a flaky soil in an entire soil mass.

Effects of Water

Water has various effects on soils, depending on the proportions of water and the particle size, shape, and chemical properties. A small amount of water tends to make sand particles stick together somewhat, generally aiding the excavation and handling of the sand. When saturated, however, most sands behave like highly viscous fluids, moving easily under stress due to gravity or other sources.

The effect of the variation of water content is generally most dramatic in fine-grained soils. These will change from rocklike solids when totally dry to virtual fluids when supersaturated.

Another water-related property is the relative ease with which water flows through or can be extracted from the soil mass, called permeability. Coarse-grained soils tend to be rapid draining and highly permeable. Fine-grained soils tend to be nondraining or impervious, and may literally seal out flowing water.

Plasticity of Fine-Grained Soils

Table A.1 describes the Atterberg limits for fine-grained soils. These are the water content limits, or boundaries, between four stages of structural character of the soil. An important property for such soils is the *plasticity index*, which is the numeric difference between the liquid limit and the plastic limit.

A major physical distinction between clays and silts is the range of the plastic state, referred to as the relative plasticity of the soil. Clays typically have a considerable plastic range while silts have practically none, going almost directly from the semisolid state to the liquid state. The plasticity chart, shown in Figure A.3, is used to classify clays and silts on the basis of two properties: liquid limit and plasticity. The diagonal line on the chart is the classification boundary between the two soil types.

Soil Structures

Soil structures may be classified in many ways. A major distinction is made between soils considered *cohesive* and those considered *cohesionless*. Cohesionless soils consist primarily of sand and gravel where there is no significant bonding of the discrete soil particles. The addition of a small amount of fine-

TABLE A.1 ATTERBERG LIMITS FOR WATER CONTENT IN FINE-GRAINED SOILS

Description of Structural Character of the Soil Mass	Analogous Material and Behavior	Water Content Limit
Liquid	Thick soup: flows or is very easily deformed	
		Liquid limit: w_L
Plastic	Thick frosting or toothpaste: retains shape but is easily deformed without cracking	Magnitude of range is *plasticity index*: I_p
		Plastic limit: w_P
Semisolid	Cheddar cheese or hard caramel candy: takes permanent deformation but cracks	
		Shrinkage limit: w_S
Solid	Hard cookie: crumbles up if deformed	(Least volume attained upon drying out)

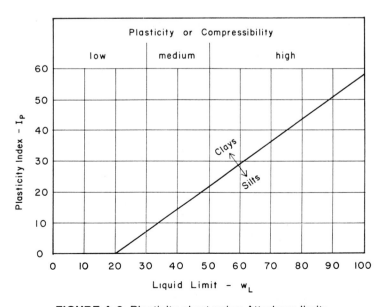

FIGURE A.3 Plasticity chart using Atterberg limits

grained material will cause a cohesionless soil to form a weakly bonded mass when dry, but the bonding will virtually disappear with a small percentage of moisture. As the percentage of fine materials is increased, the soil mass becomes progressively more cohesive, tending to retain some defined shape right up to the fully saturated, liquid consistency.

The extreme cases of cohesive and cohesionless soils are represented, respectively, by a pure clay and a pure, or clean, sand. Typically, soils range between these extremes, which are useful in defining boundary conditions for classification.

Sands

For a clean sand, the structural nature of the soil mass will largely be determined by three properties: the particle shape (well rounded versus angular), the nature of size gradation (well graded, gap graded, or uniform), and the density or degree of *compaction* of the soil mass.

The density of a sand deposit relates to how closely the particles fit together and is essentially measured by the void ratio or percentage. The actions of water, vibration, shock, or compressive force will tend to pack the particles into tighter (denser) arrangements. Thus, the same sand particles may produce strikingly different soil deposits as a result of density variation.

Table A.2 provides the range of density classifications that are commonly used in describing sand deposits, ranging from very loose to very dense. The general character of the deposit and the typical range of usuable bearing strength are shown as they relate to density. As mentioned previously, however, the effective nature of the soil depends on additional considerations, principally the particle shape and the size gradation.

TABLE A.2 AVERAGE PROPERTIES OF COHESIONLES SOILS

Relative Density	Blow Count, N, blows/ft	Void Ratio, e	Simple Field Test with $\frac{1}{2}$-in. Diameter Rod	Usable Bearing Strength	
				k/ft^2	kPa
Loose	< 10	0.65–0.85	Easily pushed in by hand	0–1.0	0–50
Medium	10–30	0.35–0.65	Easily driven in by hammer	1.0–2.0	50–100
Dense	30–50	0.25–0.50	Driven in by repeated hammer blows	1.5–3.0	75–150
Very dense	> 50	0.2–0.35	Barely penetrated by repeated hammer blows	2.5–4.0	125–200

Clays and Silts

Many physical and chemical properties affect the structural character of clays. Major considerations are the particle size, the particle shape, and whether the particles are organic or inorganic. The amount of water in a clay deposit has a very significant effect on its structural nature, changing it from a rocklike material when dry to a viscous fluid when saturated.

The property of a clay corresponding to the density of sand is its consistency, varying from very soft to very hard. The general nature of clays and their typical, usable bearing strengths as they relate to consistency are shown in Table A.3.

Another major property of fine-grained soils (clays and silts) is their relative *plasticity*. This was previously discussed in terms of the Atterberg limit (Table A.1), and the classification was made using the plasticity chart shown in Figure A.3.

Most fine-grained soils contain both silt and clay, and the predominant character of the soil is evaluated in terms of various measured properties, most significant of which is the plasticity index. Thus, an identification as "silty" usually indicates a lack of plasticity (crumbly, friable, etc.), while that of "claylike" or "clayey" usually indicates some significant degree of plasticity (moldable without fracture, even when only partly wet).

Special Soil Structures

Various special soil structures are formed by actions that help produce the original soil deposit or work on the deposit after it is in place. Coarse-grained soils with a small percentage of fine-grained material may develop arched

TABLE A.3 AVERAGE PROPERTIES OF COHESIVE SOILS

Consistency	Unconfined Compressive Stength, k/ft^2	Simple Field Test by Handling of an Undisturbed Sample	Usable Bearing Strength	
			k/ft^2	kPa
Very soft	<0.5	Oozes between fingers when squeezed	0	0
Soft	0.5–1.0	Easily modeled by fingers	0.5–1.0	25–50
Medium	1.0–2.0	Molded by moderately hard squeezing	1.0–1.5	50–75
Stiff	2.0–3.0	Barely molded by strong squeezing	1.0–2.0	50–100
Very stiff	3.0–4.0	Barely dented by very hard squeezing	1.5–3.0	75–150
Hard	4.0 or more	Dented only with a sharp instrument	3.0+	150+

arrangements of the cemented coarse particles, resulting in a soil structure that is called *honeycombed*. Organic decomposition, electrolytic action, or other factors can cause soils consisting of mixtures of bulky and flaky particles to form highly voided soils that are called *flocculent*. The nature of the formation of these soils is shown in Figure A.4. Water deposited silts and sands, such as those found at the bottom of dry streams or ponds, should be suspected of this condition if the tested void ratio is quite high.

Honeycombed and flocculent soils may have considerable static strength and be quite adequate for foundation purposes provided no unstabilizing effects are anticipated. A sudden, unnatural increase in the water content, such as that due to the introduction of continuous irrigation, or some significant shock or vibration may disturb the fragile bonding, however, resulting in major consolidation of the soil deposit. This can produce substantial settlement of ground surfaces, pavements, or structures if the affected soil mass is extensive.

Structural Behavior of Soils

Behavior under stress is usually quite different for the two basic soil types: sand and clay. Sand has little resistance to compressive stress unless it is confined. Consider the difference in behavior of a handful of dry sand and sand rammed into a strong container. Clay, on the other hand, has some resistance to both compression and tension in an unconfined condition, extending to its liquid consistency. If a hard, dry clay is pulverized, however, it becomes similar to loose sand until some water is added.

The basic structural behavior and significant properties that affect it for the two extreme soil types are summarized as follows.

Sand.   Has little compression resistance without some confinement. Principal stress mechanism is shear resistance (interlocking particles grinding to-

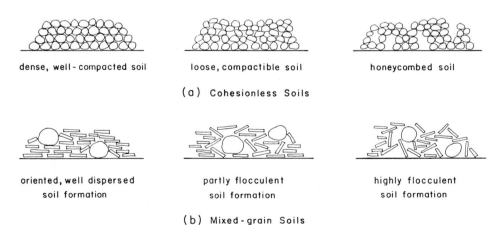

dense, well-compacted soil   loose, compactible soil   honeycombed soil

(a) Cohesionless Soils

oriented, well dispersed   partly flocculent   highly flocculent
soil formation   soil formation   soil formation

(b) Mixed-grain Soils

FIGURE A.4 Arrangements of soil particles in various soil structures

gether). Important properties are penetration resistance to a driven object, unit density, grain shape, predominant grain size and size gradation, and a derived property called the *angle of internal friction*. Some reduction in capacity with high (saturated or supersaturated) water content.

Clay.   Principal stress resistance in tension (cohesive tendency). Confinement generally of concern only in very soft, wet clays that may ooze or flow if compressed or relieved of confinement. Important properties are the tested unconfined compressive strength, liquid limit, plasticity index, and relative consistency (soft to hard).

These are, of course, the extreme limits or outer boundaries in terms of soil types. Most soils are neither pure clays nor clean sands, possessing some characteristics of both of the basic extremes.

A.4   SOIL CLASSIFICATION AND IDENTIFICATION

Soil classification and identification must account for a number of properties in precise categorizing a particular soil sample. Many systems exist and are used by various groups with different concerns. The three most widely used systems are the triangular textural system used by the U.S. Department of Agriculture; the AASHO system, named for its developer, the American Association of State Highway Officials; and the unified system, which is used in foundation engineering.

The unified system pertains to properties that are of major concern in stress and deformation behaviors, excavation and dewatering problems, stability under loads, and other issues of concern to foundation designers. The triangular textural system relates to problems of erosion, water retention, ease of cultivation, etc. The AASHO system primarily concerns the effectiveness of soils for use as base materials for pavements, both as natural deposits and as fill materials.

Figure. A.5 shows the triangular textural system, given in graphic form, which permits easy identification of the limits used to distinguish the named soil types. The property used is strictly grain-size percentage, which makes the identification somewhat approximate since there are potential overlaps between fine sand and silt and between silt and clay. For agricultural purposes, this is of less concern than it may be in foundation engineering.

Use of the textural graph consists of finding the percentage of the three basic soil types in a sample and projecting the three edge points to an intersection point that falls in one of the named groups. For example, a soil having 46% sand (possibly including some gravel), 21% silt, and 33% clay would fall in the group called ''sandy clay loam.'' However, it would be close to the border of ''clay loam'' and would fall somewhere between the two soil types in actual nature.

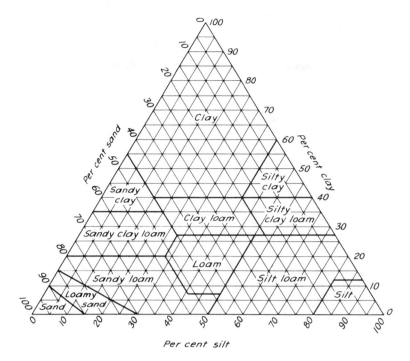

FIGURE A.5 Triangular textural classification chart used by the U.S. Department of Agriculture

One use of the triangular graph is to observe the extent to which percentages of the various materials affect the essential nature of soil. A sand, for example, must be relatively clean (free of fines) to be considered as such. With as much as 60% sand and only 40% clay, a soil is considered essentially a clay.

The AASHO system is shown in Table A.4. The three basic items of data used are grain-size analysis, the liquid limit, and plasticity index, the latter two properties relating only to fine-grained soils. On the basis of this data the soil is located by group, and its general usefulness as a base for paving is rated.

The unified system is shown in Figure 2.6. It consists of categorizing the soil into one of 15 groups, each identified by a two-letter symbol. As with the AASHO system, the primary data used includes the grain-size analysis, liquid limit, and plasticity index. The unified system is not significantly superior to the AASHO system in terms of its database, but it provides more distinct identification of soils pertaining to their general structural behavior.

Building codes and engineering handbooks often use some simplified system of grouping soil types for the purpose of regulating foundation design and construction.

TABLE A.4 AMERICAN ASSOCIATION OF STATE HIGHWAY OFFICIALS CLASSIFICATION OF SOILS AND SOIL AGGREGATE MIXTURES—AASHO DESIGNATION M-145

General Classification[a]	Granular Materials (35% or Less Passing No. 200)							Silt-Clay Materials (More than 35% Passing No. 200)				
	A-1		A-3	A-2				A-4	A-5	A-6	A-7 A-7-5	A-7 A-7-6
Group Classification	A-1-a	A-1-b		A-2-4	A-2-5	A-2-6	A-2-7					
Sieve analysis, % passing:												
No. 10	50 max											
No. 40	30 max	50 max	51 min									
No. 200	15 max	25 max	10 max	35 max	35 max	35 max	35 max	36 min	36 min	36 min	36 min	36 min
Characteristics of fraction passing No. 40:												
Liquid limit				40 max	41 min	40 max	41 min	40 max	41 min	40 max	41 min	41 min
Plasticity index	6 max	6 max	N.P.[b]	10 max	10 max	11 min	11 min	10 max	10 max	11 min	11 min	11 min
Usual types of significant constituent materials	Stone fragments—gravel and sand		Fine sand	Silty or clayey gravel and sand				Silty soils		Clayey soils		
General rating as subgrade	Excellent to good							Fair to poor				

[a]Classification procedure: With required test data in mind, proceed from left to right in chart; correct group will be found by process of elimination. The first group from the left consistent with the test data is the correct classification. The A-7 group is subdivided into A-7-5 or A-7-6 depending on the plastic limit. For $w_P < 30$, the classification is A-7-6; for $w_P \geqq 30$, A-7-5.

[b]N.P. denotes the nonplastic.

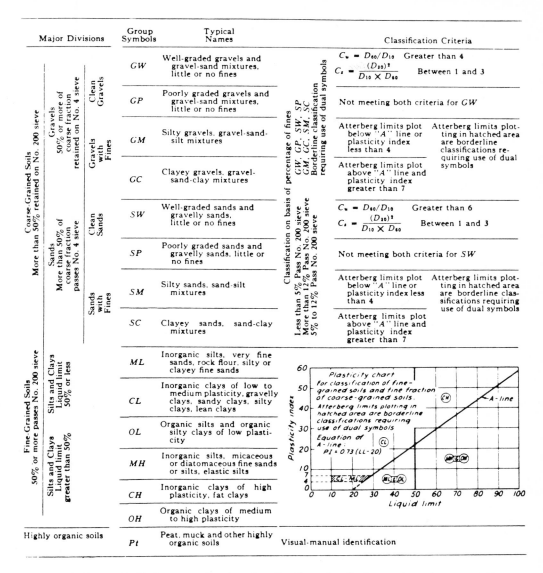

FIGURE A.6 Unified system for the classification of soils for engineering purposes (ASTM Designation D-2487)

A.5 SPECIAL SOIL PROBLEMS

A great number of special soil situations can be of major concern in site and foundation construction. Some of these are predictable on the basis of regional climate and geological conditions. A few common problems of special concern are discussed in the following material.

Expansive Soils

In climates with long dry periods, fine-grained soils often shrink to a minimum volume, sometimes producing vertical cracking in the soil masses that extends to considerable depths. When significant rainfall occurs, two phenomena occur that can produce problems for structures. The first is the rapid seepage of water into lower soil strata through the vertical cracks. The second is the swelling of the ground mass as water is absorbed, which can produce considerable upward or sideways pressure on structures.

The soil swelling can cause major stresses in foundations, especially when it occurs nonuniformly, which is the general case because of ground coverage by paving, buildings, and landscaping. Local building codes usually have provisions for design with these soils in regions where they are common.

Collapsing Soils

In general, collapsing soils are soils with large voids. The collapse mechanism is essentially one of rapid consolidation (volume reduction) as whatever tends to maintain the soil structure with the large void condition is removed or altered. Very loose sands may display such behavior when they experience drastic changes in water content or are subjected to shock or vibration.

The most common cases of soil collapse, however, are those involving soil structures in which fine-grained materials achieve a bonding or molding of cellular voids. These soils may be quite strong when relatively dry but the bonds may dissolve when the water content is significantly raised. Weakly bonded structures may also be collapsed by shock or simply by excessive compression.

The two ordinary methods of dealing with collapsing soils are to stabilize the soil by introducing materials to partly fill the void and substantially reduce the potential for collapse, or to use some means to cause the collapse to occur prior to construction. Infusion with bentonite slurry may achieve the reduction of the void without collapse. Water saturation, vibration, or overloading of the soil with fill may be used to induce collapse.

A.6 SOIL MODIFICATION

In connection with site and building construction, modifications of existing soil deposits occur in a number of ways. The recontouring of the site, placing the building on a site, covering the ground surface with large areas of paving, installing extensive plantings, and developing a continuous irrigation system all represent major changes in the site environment.

Major changes, done in a few months or years, are equivalent to ones that may take thousands of years to occur by natural causes, and the sudden disruption of the equilibrium of the geological environment is likely to have an impact; it results in readjustments that will eventually cause major changes in soil conditions, particularly those near the ground surface. The single *major* modification of site conditions, therefore, is the construction work.

In some cases, in order to achieve the construction work, compensate for disruptions caused by construction activity, or protect against future potential problems, it is necessary to make deliberate modifications of existing soils. The most common type of modification is that undertaken to stabilize or densify some soil deposit by compaction, preconsolidation, cementation, or other means. This type of modification is usually done either to improve bearing capacity and reduce settlements, or to protect against future failures in the form of surface subsidence, slippage of slopes, or erosion.

Another common modification relates to changes in the groundwater and moisture conditions. Recontouring for channelled drainage, covering the ground with buildings or paving, and major irrigation or dewatering cause changes of this type.

Deliberate changes may consist of altering the soil to change its degree of permeability of its water-retaining properties. Fine-grained materials may be leached from a mixed grain soil to make it more cohesionless and permeable. Conversely, fine materials may be introduced to make a coarse-grained soil less permeable or produce a more stable soil mass.

Except for relatively simple compaction of surface materials, all soil modifications should be undertaken only with the advice of an experienced soils consultant.

A.7 FILL

Site development typically involves the use of soils for fill. This may involve situations in which some site areas are being raised to a new finish surface (see Figure A.7a), for which a general profile is developed, by filling depres-

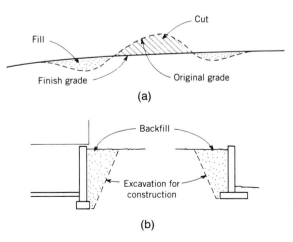

FIGURE A.7 Use of fill materials

sions with soil moved from other areas on the site that are being cut down to a new grade. If more filling than cutting is required on the site, or surface soils are unsatisfactory, fill materials will have to be brought to the site.

In most cases, selection of fill soils and their handling must be controlled to some degree. A major concern is maintaining the finished grade profile once construction is completed. This is of much greater concern if pavements or other site structures are to be placed on the fill. It is in general not good (or even not allowed by codes) to place building foundations on fill.

To avoid settlement of the surface over fills, called surface *subsidence*, it is necessary to compact the fill materials. This is usually done with equipment, working with thin layers of the fill in subsequent built-up accumulation to achieve the necessary finished grade.

The equipment and procedure used for compaction depend on the type of soil, extent of the area being compacted, and the degree of soil volume reduction desired. The latter is defined in terms of some desired degree of density compared to that of a soil with zero void. Since actual zero void is hardly feasible, a density representing from 90 to 95% of a fully compacted volume is usually acceptable as significant compaction.

The types of soils that yield to good compaction and have other properties desirable for fills are limited generally to those with predominantly coarse-grained materials and small amounts of fine-grained materials (silty sands, gravel with traces of silt and clay, etc.). Where fast draining of the fill is a requirement, the amount of fine grained materials may be strictly limited. When soils at the site do not have these properties, they may be modified; otherwise imported materials must be used.

Backfill

A special situation is that in which soil is used to fill in around construction, where overcutting of the excavation has been required (Figure A.7b). This fill is referred to as *backfill*, and its placement is often controlled for various purposes, including the following:

Prevention of subsidence of the finished grade resulting in undesirable depressions next to the construction

Prevention of damage to the construction, especially to waterproofing on surfaces of walls.

Development of perimeter drain lines

Satisfying these or other special purposes may affect the choice of fill materials, specifications for compaction, or other details of the installation. The practical thing to do is use the excavated materials where it is practical to stockpile them nearby for this purpose. However, these soils may not have the desired properties for backfill purposes, and imported materials may be required.

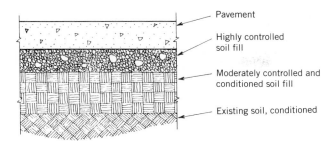

FIGURE A.8 Components of a pavement base

Fill for Pavements

Development of pavements often involves use of fill materials. Figure A.8 shows some of the typical components involved when a pavement must be built up to certain level and a stable paved surface is desired. This stacking of conditioned layers usually begins with treatment of the existing soil surface that has been exposed by cutting the original grade. This surface layer of soil may be modified by compaction, wetting, filling with some special material to increase density, etc.

The paving itself may be achieved with a variety of materials, but if it is a hard surfacing of concrete, asphalt or tiles, its direct support is usually achieved with a coarse-grained soil layer that is compacted. The degree of compaction usually relates to the form of paving and the kind of traffic being borne.

If the paved surface is developed a short distance above the undisturbed soil surface, the fill material directly supporting it may be the only base fill required. However, if the surface must be some distance above the existing cut surface, it is probably too expensive to use the special fill and some intermediate layer of fill may be used. This level-raising fill must also be controlled, again the degree depends on the type of paving and the traffic.

A further complication for fills under pavements is the common need for soil materials with good draining properties to prevent water buildup under the paving. Where this is especially critical, a piped drainage system may be installed in the supporting fill materials.

A.8 SOILS FOR LANDSCAPING

Full site development involves the controlled development of all site surfaces. Surfaces not covered by construction are typically covered by either paving or plantings. Development of hard surface paving is discussed in the preceding section; it typically requires the use of some soil materials to develop a built-up base for the actual surface pavement.

Loose Paving Materials

A special form of paving is achieved with loose soil materials—the dirt path or gravel road, for example. These may be quite crudely developed or more carefully built up as for hard paving, using all the layers shown in Figure A.8 with controlled loose surfacing replacing the hard pavement. Good surface paving as well as good sub-base materials may be found on the site, but this is most likely a fortunate accident, and some imported materials with the desired properties are usually required. Although typically described as loose, the upper layers of this form of paving are likely to be more durable if some degree of compaction is achieved with them.

Materials used for loose paving depend on the form of traffic and the appearance desired. Foot traffic may be borne on pulverized materials such as bark, brick, or clinkers. A good "dirt" path may be developed with sand and a small amount of silt to promote compaction by the traffic. Vehicular traffic usually requires the use of relatively coarse gravel, again containing a controlled amount of fine materials to promote compaction by the traffic itself.

Topsoil

Topsoils exist naturally on many sites where plant growth has occurred for many years. Principal ingredients of what is referred to as topsoil are organic materials, consisting largely of partly decomposed plant materials. Although the exact composition of topsoils varies considerably, they generally represent soils that sustain plant growth.

Development of planted areas on sites requires the use of some form of soil that can sustain plant growth. An exact specification for such a soil will relate to the plantings being installed, with special needs for particular nutrients and response to water. Very ordinary topsoils may be adequate in some cases, very highly controlled ones in others.

Where feasible, existing topsoils on a site are typically preserved—left in place if no regrading is required or stripped and stockpiled for relocation in case of major regrading. Removal may also be required where pavements or other constructions are required, since structural support is unreliable with soils of high organic content. If the existing topsoil is not all required on a site, it can sometimes be exported and sold for use on other sites.

Topsoil for site development can sometimes be produced by special treatment of existing site materials through the use of various additives. Typical additions involve fertilizers or chemicals to improve nutritive properties and various materials to reduce density and improve drainage or moisture retention.

DESIGN CHECKLISTS

Management of design is a challenging activity. If too restrictive, it tends to smother the designers and stifle creative exploration of ideas. If too loose or informal, some important factors may be ignored and the work may develop in endless loops of repetition. The following checklists consist of concise outlines of factors that should be considered (checked off) to ensure their incorporation in the design process. In a way, they amount to a summary outline of the issues presented throughout this book.

PREDESIGN

These are items that relate to the earliest involvements in a site design project. The main concern here is to gather all the critical information as early as possible and initiate the preliminary design decisions.

   1. *Collect Available Information.*
      Site survey
      Area maps, demographic studies, etc.
      Local climate and weather information
      Local and other applicable building codes
      Zoning requirements
      Title restrictions

Community master plans

Soils reports

Data for previous construction on site

Near-regional information from various agencies, (highway, agricultural, military, airports) for weather data, etc.

2. *Inspect the Site.*

Take photos:

From the site toward all sides, corners

Toward the site from all streets, vantage points

Closeups of site features: trees, streams, etc.

Views of existing construction on the site

Apparent soil failures: slides, sink holes, heavy erosion in progress, etc.

Views of any site construction in progress in the area

Take notes on:

All the photos (for identification later)

The neighbors

Traffic on adjacent streets

The character of the neighborhood

Items worth preserving

For any anticipated site design issues (major parking required, desired privacy or security, etc.)

Take samples of:

Surface soils

Unfamiliar natural growth

Water from streams, ponds, etc. (for pollution analyses)

3. *Quiz Everybody.*

The architect:

General design goals, usage needs

Size of building footprint

Orientation of building (sun, entrance, principal view, etc.)

Site traffic, parking, access points for autos and predestrians

Major exterior materials for building

General architectural style (do not use the word *style*, ask for samples)

The engineers:

Additional investigations required for anticipated site work

Soil problems, water problems

Excavations anticipated

Locations, depths, sizes, etc., of buried items (utilities, drainage elements, etc.)

Need for general preliminary grading or removal of the site surface materials (soil, vegetation, etc.)

Amount, size, weight, etc., of heavy equipment to be used on site, access required, when used

The owner:

Budget for anything beyond minimal design

Specific concerns for neighbors

Extent of maintenance planned (as it affects choice of plantings)

Site (outdoor) activities to be anticipated not included in the building design program

Local authorities:

Codes, zoning, policies regarding curb cuts, site drainage, design review bodies, community master plans

PRELIMINARY DESIGN

The items below are to be dealt with in the early stages of design when the critical concerns are communicating the problem clearly and motivating everyone involved in the project to work toward the same goals and objectives.

1. *Understand the Problem.*

   State goals and objectives clearly and share them

   Agree on specific intentions:

   Quality level of site work (minimal?, lush?)

   Preservation of site features (everybody has to agree and cooperate or this will not work)

   Specific design responsibilities and method for control of decision-making

   Design timetable

2. *Consider the Alternatives.*

   Develop all the options in sufficient detail to do comparative analyses and share this with others.

   Rank preferences and prepare to justify them.

   Ask others to select their preferences and explain why.

   Perform a benefit/cost analysis for anything that goes beyond minimum code requirements.

3. *Help the Design Team.*

   Politely suggest changes or alternatives in other plans that will improve general site situations.

   Make your specific needs and intentions clear, especially as it offers potential for conflict with others.

   Monitor the ongoing design decision process and do not raise critical needs after irreversible conditions have been established.

Anticipate the design and construction schedules and interject critical site work items into the flow:

Guard items to be preserved before anything else happens on the site.

Remove usable topsoils before the general preliminary grading for construction work.

Define needs for special installations, such as large trees, heavy water-using plantings, plantings requiring major sunlight, etc.

Analyze thoroughly the detailed requirements for barrier-free access and other code items, and share with the team before site form is fully developed.

LANDSCAPING CONCERNS

These issues relate to the development of the general landscaping, with emphasis on plantings and planting-related constructions.

1. *Existing Conditions*

Evaluate existing plantings for preservation.

Are they overgrown or otherwise inappropriate for the intended site use?

Are they healthy and likely to endure; especially under the new site conditions?

What extreme or unusual measures may be necessary for their preservation and protection during the construction work?

What site work may they interfere with, and who should be given early notice during the design and advance warning for planning of construction work?

What special construction or consideration may be required to protect them?

What other site elements may be desirable for use in the finished site development?

Natural earth forms, especially at edges merging with neighboring properties

Rock outcroppings—to be left as is or merged into planned developments?

Large rocks—to be stockpiled and used in finished work?

Natural water features: streams, ponds, drainage channels

Views, both good and bad

Can surface soils be removed, relocated, stored, and used for the finish surface development? If so, where can they be stockpiled for protection during the construction?

Can smaller trees or other existing plants be dug up and saved for re-planting in the finished site?

2. *Choice of Plantings*

Appropriate to the local climate, natural local growth, plantings in the neighborhood, local requirements, etc.

Appropriate in terms of anticipated degree of care that may be provided

Related to miscellaneous site design concerns:

Blocking of views from buildings, by neighbors, of cars emerging into street traffic, for security, etc.

Blocking of breezes—pro or con

Feasibility of irrigation

Screening of some proposed site features: parking, service areas, trash, surface utility elements, etc.

Growth patterns and anticipated maximum size

Blocking of solar access on the site or for the neighbors (many codes now control this).

Effects of root propagation, especially for trees and large shrubs in confined areas (may require root barriers in some locations)

Availability from local sources

3. *Pavements and Ground Covers*

Choice of pavements appropriate to the traffic:

Structurally adequate, especially for vehicles

Surfacing compatible with other landscaping materials; especially ground covers

Use of loose or open pavings to reduce water runoff and hold ground moisture

Ground cover appropriate to site functions:

Use for traffic-bearing areas, play space, etc.

Use to inhibit or control traffic

Use to reduce erosion of slopes

General relations to site drainage

4. *Landscape Construction*

Choice of materials to compliment exterior materials of buildings

Double use of construction:

Edged plantings areas as traffic dividers

Decorative lighting for functional purposes

5. *Landscape Drainage*

Investigate drainage created by soil forms for the landscape development.

Consider the impact of drainage from paved areas on planted areas.

Where possible, integrate site drainage with building storm drainage.

PARKING AND CIRCULATION

These are some general concerns for the development of site circulation, surface parking and various site features that relate to the problems of using site parking.

1. *Access*

   Can parking areas be easily found by strangers arriving at the site?

   Is the traffic path to the parking crossed by many other traffic paths?

   If access is controlled, how is control achieved:

   Key-operated gates? Signs only? Clear alternatives in the traffic paths?

   Is access clear and controlled for various special purposes?
      Postal and other delivery services
      Service vehicles, trash trucks, etc.
      Firefighting equipment

   Does pedestrian access relate to public walks, presently used neighborhood traffic paths, and public transportation?

2. *Parking Stall Sizes*

   What size vehicles must be provided for?

   Is a single size stall appropriate for the entire parking lot?

   Is space available for the required number of handicapped parking stalls and any associated access ramps, etc.?

3. *Lot Form*

   Is right angle parking required? (Mostly only for two-way access drive traffic.)

   What forms of parking are possible?
      Parallel parking along site roads or driveways
      Multiple end-to-end stalls for long-term parking

   Can a large amount of required parking be divided into several lots to avoid the asphalt wasteland?

   Is the space for development of some landscaping within the parking lot?

   How does parking location relate to building points of entry or other site elements?

FINAL DESIGN REVIEW

The concerns here relate to the verification and approvals required for the design work before construction begins. This is a highly variable situation, depending on the project nature and size, the local agencies with approval authority, and the nature of the contracts for the construction work.

1. *Specific Performance Factors*

   Site surface drainage analysis for runoff from precipitation and irrigation

   Shading analysis for solar access by neighbors, using maximum growth sizes for trees

   Environmental impact studies for traffic on local streets

2. *Code Compliance*

   Satisfaction of all codes with jurisdiction:
   Local building codes and zoning ordinances
   State codes for health, handicapped requirements, energy use, etc.
   Federal standards for safety, access, etc.

3. *Design Integration*

   Verification of coordination of all aspects of the site design, especially when work is done by many different people: architect, site planner, landscape architect, engineers for site construction and foundations, utility companies involved in installation of buried elements on site, etc.

APPENDIX C

PROPERTIES OF COMMON GEOMETRIC FORMS

For various purposes in site design work it is necessary to compute quantities for geometric forms. Examples of such computations are those required to find the total linear length for a property line fence, the surface area of a portion of open ground for planting, and the volume of an excavation. Such elements may be considerably irregular in shape, but often consist simply of ordinary geometric forms, or at the most, of multiples of simple forms.

Even very irregular forms may often be broken down for reasonable approximation into multiples of simple forms. This may be reasonably adequate for preliminary estimates or even for final work. Use of presently available computer-aided procedures makes this less useful for final design work, but simple hand computations for preliminary work are still valuable.

Figure C.1 presents properties of a number of common planar geometric forms. Figure C.2 presents some common three-dimensional shapes with data for determining surface areas and volumes.

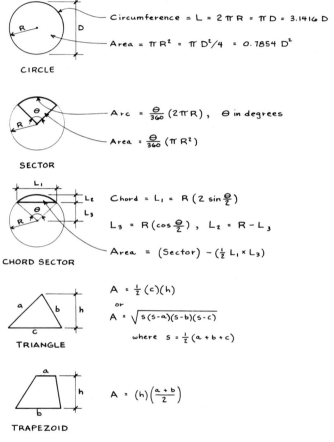

FIGURE C.1

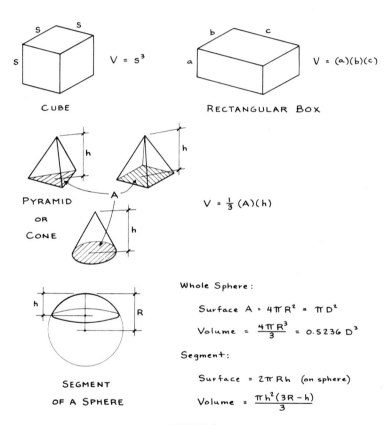

$V = s^3$

CUBE

$V = (a)(b)(c)$

RECTANGULAR BOX

PYRAMID
OR
CONE

$V = \frac{1}{3}(A)(h)$

SEGMENT
OF A SPHERE

Whole Sphere :

Surface $A = 4\pi R^2 = \pi D^2$

Volume $= \frac{4\pi R^3}{3} = 0.5236\, D^3$

Segment :

Surface $= 2\pi R h$ (on sphere)

Volume $= \frac{\pi h^2 (3R - h)}{3}$

FIGURE C.2

STUDY AIDS

The materials in this section are intended to provide the readers with some means to measure their comprehension of the information in this book. It is recommended that upon completion of an individual chapter, the materials given here for that chapter be utilized to determine what has been learned. Answers to the questions are given at the end of this section.

WORDS AND TERMS

Using the glossary, index, and text of each chapter indicated, review the meaning of the following words and terms.

Chapter 1

Site
Site design
Building site
Site edges
Building/site relations

Chapter 2

Site development
Architect

Landscape architect
Civil engineer
Planner
Geotechnical consultant
Excavation
Grading
Regrading
Micro-site
Macro-site
Topology

Survey
Contour
Access
Building footprint

Chapter 3

Surveying
Site survey
Land surveyor
Easement
Geotechnical survey
Cartography
Benchmark
Plot plan
Recontouring
Grading plan
Finished grade
Construction plan
Zoning ordinance
Title
Property line
Building code
Building permit
Minimal
Optimal

Chapter 4

Design problem
Site planning
Traffic
Traffic path
Barrier-free access
Surface parking
Structure parking
Parking lot
Parking stall
Handicapped parking
Earth berm
Visible site

Invisible site
Management of site materials

Chapter 5

Siting a building
Building base
Backfill
Building services
Building/site spatial continuity

Chapter 6

Cut
Fill
Subsurface materials
Grading
Finished grade
Surface drainage
Erosion
Runoff
Watershed
Geotextile
Channelling
Site edge constraints
Building footprint

Chapter 7

Landscaping
Site as a viewed object
Plantings
Ground cover
Planter
Irrigation

Chapter 8

Site construction
Stability of slopes
Slope angle limit
Sheet piling
Soldier beam

Lagging

Raker

Drilled-in anchor

Pavement

Paver

Slab on grade

Asphalt

Pavement base

Framed pavement

Compaction

Curb

Loose-laid retaining wall

Cantilever retaining wall

Gravity retaining wall

Overturning effect

Shear key for footing

Channel

Tunnel

Sewer

Ramp

Chapter 9

Illumination

General illumination

Task lighting

Acoustics

Security

Safety

Life safety

Questions

Chapter 1

1. What is site design?
2. Who does site design?

Chapter 2

1. What are the primary user functions that must be dealt with in the construction for a building site?
2. What are the basic aspects of site design work?
3. What is meant by the term *micro-site*?
4. What is meant by the term *macro-site*?
5. Besides the legal owner of the property, for whom may it be proper to design a site?

Chapter 3

1. What is meant by the term *existing site*?
2. Why may it be important to protect the existing site?
3. Why is it sometimes difficult to fully define the site design ''problem'' before performing a thorough investigation of the site?
4. Besides the dimensional location of property lines, what major elements usually appear on a site survey, as prepared by a land surveyor to be recorded as a legal document?
5. What is the difference between a site survey and a site plan?

6. Other than the identification of the owner, what is the major purpose of a title for a piece of land (site)?

7. Why are building code requirements not good design objectives in most cases?

Chapter 4

1. What are the primary purposes in developing a clear statement of a design "problem"?

2. What basic data about a specific type of motor vehicle most affects the planning of site traffic paths and parking?

3. Why is it difficult to establish a single, ideal size for a parking stall for an automobile?

4. What are some principal physical features required for the construction of traffic paths for: a) Pedestrians? b) Automobiles?

5. What can be done to avoid the vast wasteland appearance of large parking lots?

6. Although a single parking stall for an automobile may be only about 150 ft^2, a parking lot may need to have a total area of as much as 350 sq ft per vehicle parked. Why is this necessary?

7. Besides the lot itself, what major site elements are usually required to accommodate persons arriving at a building by automobile?

8. Designing the viewed site is complicated by the various conditions for viewing. What are some major viewing situations that must usually be considered?

9. What are some major typical elements that must be dealt with in managing the shared space of the invisible site?

10. Why is it desirable to balance the cuts and fills when regrading a site?

11. Even when the level of the finished grade is not substantially changed from that of the existing site, it may be necessary to remove considerable soil from the site. What are some reasons for this?

Chapter 5

1. What is meant by the term *siting the building*?

2. How can the size and shape of the site affect the planning of the building?

3. How can the building plan affect the planning of the site?

4. What factors influence the development of the means of access to the site?

5. How does the location of sewer mains potentially affect the positioning of the building on the site?

6. What are the two primary changes of a site that are unavoidable when a building is to be placed on the site?

Chapter 6

1. Even though the cut and fill required to modify a site surface may be reasonably balanced volumetrically, it may be necessary to remove considerable material from the site. What are some reasons for this?
2. What are some differences between finished surfaces that are cut down and those that are built up with fill?
3. Developing the finished site surface as a modification from the existing surface is often achieved in stages. Why is this?
4. What are some of the major physical problems to be treated in developing the site drainage?

Chapter 7

1. Landscaping work is sometimes considered essentially a cosmetic effort, yet landscape *design* has a broader context. What makes this so?
2. Why is the timing of the work sometimes a critical issue in the design and construction work of landscape development?
3. Landscaping work generally deals most directly with the site surface materials, yet concerns for deeper levels of ground materials may affect design. What are some reasons for this?
4. Where extensive site construction work is planned, it is often a considerable challenge to preserve any existing plantings. Why is this so?
5. A major part of landscape design deals with the nature of the viewed site. What are some other major concerns?
6. Rather than merely being stuck into the ground, plantings are sometimes developed in some form of container. What are some reasons for this?
7. What are the basic requirements for providing of successful plant growth?
8. What are the problems involved in ensuring proper water supplies for plantings?

Chapter 8

1. What is the single most critical factor in dealing with design for slope control?
2. Besides the downward slipping of the soil mass due to the effects of gravity, what is the greatest cause of soil loss on a sloped surface?
3. What are the two primary properties generally desired for the soil base for a pavement?
4. Concrete pavements developed as slabs on grade do not generally function as spanning structures. If so, why is steel reinforcement usually provided for them?
5. What is the primary reason for providing closely spaced, discontinuous joints in concrete pavements?

6. What is the basic reason for using a framed pavement?

7. Loose-laid retaining walls lack structural resistance due to the unbonded nature of their construction. However, the open joints present an advantage in dealing with one potential force effect. What is that effect?

8. What does a cantilever retaining wall cantilever from?

9. Major construction of drainage channels on a site must usually be coordinated with off-site concerns. Why is this?

10. Why is it desirable to have a certain minimum number of steps in a stair?

Chapter 9

1. Other than the type of lamp and fixture used, what most influences the nature of illumination provided by a general site lighting system?

2. What is the best way to reduce the undesirable effects on site occupants of a noise source that is located on the site?

3. How can good site planning reduce the need for excessive signage on the site?

4. What is generally meant by a ''barrier'' when the term barrier–free is used?

5. How does the provision of a generally barrier-free site environment improve conditions for persons with generally no limited physical capacities?

6. As we generally use the term in site design, what does *safety* really mean?

Answers to the Questions

Chapter 1

1. The work necessary in determining all the work to be done for the development of a site for some planned purpose.

2. Whoever gets the assignment. Many different design professionals contend for the job.

Chapter 2

1. Site surface drainage, placing the building on the site, site edge development, site lighting, sound control, air quality, fire safety, security, etc.

2. Investigation of existing conditions, engineering design for site construction, landscape design, building foundation design.

3. The site itself and issues that are internal to the site.

4. The world outside the site.

5. The neighbors, passersby, birds, roving animals, butterflies, etc.

Chapter 3

1. The condition of the site before any planned work on it begins.
2. To preserve anything on it that needs to be saved.
3. The precise nature of the information required from the investigations will be partly affected by the design goals and objectives, and vice versa.
4. Elevations of points on the site, identification of adjacent streets and properties, existing buildings, and other features on the site.
5. A site survey establishes the conditions on the site at the time of the survey. Plans are made to illustrate proposed changes.
6. To describe the property accurately and locate it precisely on the surface of the earth.
7. Code requirements are mostly of the character of minimum adequacy (least acceptable), not of the character of optimal (best you can get).

Chapter 4

1. To inform an intelligent design and be sure the designers and site owners agree on the goals.
2. Plan dimensions of the vehicle and its minimum turning radius. Wheel loads also affect the form of pavement required.
3. There is no "standard" size automobile.
4. a) Barrier-free, nonslippery surfaces, clear indications of pathways to specific places. b) Adequate width and turning radius for vehicles, clear directions for traffic control.
5. Break them up into smaller lots, insert large plantings, screen separate areas with walls or earth forms.
6. Site space is also required for drives into the lot, between stalls, for turnaround areas, etc.
7. Access drive into the site and the parking lot, walking paths from the lot to site features (the buildings, etc.).
8. Night and day, seasons of the year, site users and people off the site, views from inside the buildings on the site.
9. Plant roots, building basements and foundations, buried piping, wiring, tunnels, vaults, and other underground elements.
10. To avoid major removal or importation of soil materials for the site.
11. Existing materials may be undesirable or major excavations for construction may be required.

Chapter 5

1. Placing the building on the site, horizontally and vertically, and relating it to site features, site edges, views, sun, etc.
2. Restricting the outer dimensions and shape of the building, mostly when the building covers a major part of the site surface.

3. By restricting the amount of site space available, by requiring considerations for access to the building, and by requiring major shape changes
   for the site surface.
4. Location of streets, allowable locations for curb cuts, existing sidewalks, locations of site features to be preserved, and legal requirements
   for barrier-free access.
5. The need for slope of sewer piping to facilitate drainage by gravity flow
   may affect the placement of the building vertically with regard to the
   elevation of the sewer main or horizontally with regard to the distance
   from the sewer main.
6. The building becomes a new site object, displacing some existing space
   or objects. The building needs to be accessed and generally requires
   other site services (for parking, etc.).

Chapter 6

1. The existing site materials may not be usable for the site development
   intended. Considerable excavation may be required for the site and
   building construction. Topsoil may be stripped off and stockpiled for
   use in final landscaping work.
2. Cut surfaces expose subsurface soils, which must be considered for their
   role as surface materials. Fills tend to consolidate (shrink volumetrically) over time, which presents problems, especially for any construction placed on them.
3. To facilitate the various stages of the construction work.
4. Developing the geometry of the site surface to provide for proper drainage, preventing erosion of surface soils, channelling of drainage to desired points, and disposing of the drained water, usually off the site.

Chapter 7

1. The landscaping elements on the site may be limited, but the view of
   the ''landscape'' encompasses the whole site, everything on it, the site
   edges, and the world beyond. It is therefore not usually possible to see
   the site landscape outside the context of the whole view.
2. The finished landscape is usually done last, but some preparations for
   it must be provided in the very early stages of construction. Particular
   concerns are for preservation of site features, existing trees, and topsoil.
3. Roots for large plants will penetrate to lower soils. Irrigation may cause
   problems in lower soil formations. Decomposition or other ongoing
   changes in lower soils may cause movements of the ground surface.
4. They may be damaged during the construction work. Covering the site
   surface with construction can starve existing plants by choking off air
   and draining away surface water. Excavations can cut off plant roots.
5. General concerns for the *participation* of people in the landscape, using
   site features, gaining access to the buildings, etc.

6. Control of their spread, protection of underground elements from root intrusion, and protection of the plants from traffic.
7. Selecting the correct plants, placing them properly on the site, and providing adequate water, air, sunlight, nourishment, frost protection, etc.
8. Providing for the needs of different plants, avoiding erosion, avoiding groundwater intrusion in basements, and using water in times of drought.

Chapter 8

1. The angle of the slope.
2. Erosion from runoff of precipitation.
3. Solid, nondeforming support and good drainage to prevent water accumulation under the pavement.
4. Primarily to resist shrinkage cracks.
6. The ground surface beneath the pavement cannot be relied on for support.
7. Buildup of water in the soil mass behind the wall.
8. Its footing.
9. Drainage from the site goes to somewhere off the site. This becomes even more critical in terms of the concentration of the flow when it is collected into constructed channels.
10. To make the stair more visible, reducing the likelihood that people will not notice it and will trip on the steps.

Chapter 9

1. The height and spacing of the fixtures.
2. Keep them as far apart as possible; otherwise, use site construction placed between them.
3. Make site features visible and their functions obvious, especially for traffic paths.
4. Something that impedes access, usually by persons with some physical disfunction or limited capacity such as being in a wheelchair, being very old, being blind, lacking language skills, etc.
5. It generally increases the level of safety for use of the site.
6. Life safety, regarding lack of risk to humans.

INDEX